ॐ

SANSKRIT DEVANAGARI FONT

Open Type Design, Indic Shaping & Spell Check

AF515895

Ashwini Kumar Aggarwal

जय गुरुदेव

© 2021, Author

ISBN13: 978-81-950754-8-5 Paperback Edition
ISBN13: 978-81-950754-7-8 Hardbound Edition
ISBN13: 978-81-950754-4-7 Digital Edition

This work is licensed under a Creative Commons Attribution 4.0 International License. Please visit
https://creativecommons.org/licenses/by/4.0/

Title: **Sanskrit Devanagari Font**
SubTitle: **Open Type Design, Indic Shaping & Spell Check**
Author: **Ashwini Kumar Aggarwal**

Printed and Published by
Devotees of Sri Sri Ravi Shankar Ashram
34 Sunny Enclave, Devigarh Road,
Patiala 147001, Punjab, India

https://advaita56.weebly.com/
The Art of Living Centre

https://www.artofliving.org/

21st January 2021, Dipanshu at TIET 34th Convocation, Guruji's 1st Satsang after Bangalore Ashram reopens on 2nd Jan 2021
Pausha Shukla Paksha Ashtami, Ashwini Nakshatra, Uttarayana
Vikram Samvat 2077 Pramadi, Saka Era 1942 Sharvari

1st Edition January 2021

जय गुरुदेव

Dedication

Sri Sri Ravi Shankar

who infuses Faith in all of Creation

Blessing

All that you can do is to raise the level of Sattva. And then when Sattva's level is high, we have to wait one moment, any moment knowledge can dawn there.

All that you can do to have sunlight in this room, is to open the curtains and keep the windows open. And when dawn comes, it just dawns. You have the sunlight inside.

Sri Sri Ravi Shankar
A discourse on Yogasara Upanishad

Preface

Boys hope and achieve the impossible.

A single Soul can change the landscape and the fortunes of the entire planet.

Men may come and men may go, but the boyish Spirit remains alive and indomitable, nay incorrigible.

Prayer

शान्तिपाठः

ॐ सह नाववतु । सह नौ भुनक्तु । सह वीर्यं करवावहै ।

तेजस्वि नावधीतमस्तु मा विद्विषावहै ॥

ॐ शान्तिः शान्तिः शान्तिः ॥

oṃ saha nāvavatu | saha nau bhunaktu | saha vīryaṃ karavāvahai | tejasvi nāvadhītamastu mā vidviṣāvahai ||

oṃ śānti śānti śāntiḥ ||

Peace Invocation

O Pure Loving Grace!

May we be taken care of along with our family and friends.
May we enjoy socializing and eating together.
May we support each other's vision and growth.
May our intellect be open to new ideas and changing trends.
May we spend more time in praise than abuse, may we talk of each other's virtues rather than harp on vices.

Peace in our heart, in our body and in our environs.

Technical Terms

Character = a Unicode space holder. E.g. U+0905

Glyph = a Symbol or Sign or Ligature that is drawn in the Unicode Character space. E.g. अ

Ligature = a combination of Glyphs. E.g. ङ्क

Symbol = an independent Glyph. E.g. क

Sign = a dependent Glyph, that attaches to another Glyph. E.g. ◌ी

Ayogavaha = an extra nasal or breath sound produced during speaking. For Devanagari texts, it is ideal to have written symbols for such sounds. E.g. ◌ं

Allographs = Language specific glyph change is known as allograph.

Private Use Block

This is an important section in Unicode, whereby we can directly see and insert any glyph of the font using MS Word. So it is a must in a Vedic Sanskrit font Sanskrit 2020/Advaita Sanskrit, that has many conjuncts and alternate letters/glyphs.

Helps in Teaching Grammar.

E.g. U+1CE9+0902 Gomukha Anusvara that should combine with Bindu. ᳩं ᳪं ᳫं ᳬं ᳮं ᳩँ ᳪँ ᳫँ ᳬँ ᳮँ

E.g. Rigveda Accented Numeral. १॒॑ ३॒॑

E.g. U+1CEA+0902+1CED Gomukha Anusvara that should combine with Bindu andTiryak. ᳪं᳭

E.g. U+A8F3+0951 Long Anusvara that should combine with Accents.
ꣳ॑ ꣳ॒

E.g. Half Forms that otherwise cannot be typed. व् ख् ग् ह् ठ्

E.g. Stylistic or Alternate Letters that otherwise cannot be typed.
प्र ट ह रु रू त्त

E.g. Conjuncts. ञ्छ्रु स्स्य

E.g. Top Repha etc. ꣸ = ॉ ॉः

Devanāgari Half Forms

Independent Half Forms क्‍ख्‍ग्‍घ्‍च्‍ज्‍झ्‍ञ्‍ण्‍त्‍थ्‍ध्‍न्‍प्‍फ्‍ब्‍भ्‍म्‍य्‍र्‍ल्‍व्‍श्‍ष्‍स्‍

Half Forms customarily with Halant ङ् छ् ट् ठ् ड् ढ् द् ह्

Vedic Sanskrit ळ्‍ ळ्ह्‍

Half Conjuncts क्ष्‍ ज्ञ्‍

Open Type Design in Font Editor uses code HalfForms (half)

- Zero Width Joiner character U+200D
- Replacing resultant glyph with suitable glyph from Private Use Area block

क + ◌् + $200D = क् → क्‍	च + ◌् + $200D = क् → च्‍	ट + ◌् + $200D = ट्
ख + ◌् + $200D = ख् → ख्‍	छ + ◌् + $200D = छ्	ठ + ◌् + $200D = ठ्
ग + ◌् + $200D = ग् → ग्‍	ज + ◌् + $200D = क् → ज्‍	ड + ◌् + $200D = ड्
घ + ◌् + $200D = घ् → घ्‍	झ + ◌् + $200D = क् → झ्‍	ढ + ◌् + $200D = ढ्
ङ + ◌् + $200D = ङ्	ञ + ◌् + $200D = क् → ञ्‍	ण + ◌् + $200D = ण् → ण्‍
त + ◌् + $200D = क् → त्‍	प + ◌् + $200D = प् → प्‍	य + ◌् + $200D = य् → य्‍
थ + ◌् + $200D = क् → थ्‍	फ + ◌् + $200D = क् → फ्‍	र + ◌् + $200D = र् → र्‍
द + ◌् + $200D = द्	ब + ◌् + $200D = क् → ब्‍	ल + ◌् + $200D = ल् → ल्‍
ध + ◌् + $200D = क् → ध्‍	भ + ◌् + $200D = क् → भ्‍	व + ◌् + $200D = व् → व्‍
न + ◌् + $200D = क् → न्‍	म + ◌् + $200D = क् → म्‍	
श + ◌् + $200D = श् → श्‍	ळ + ◌् + $200D = ळ्	क्ष + ◌् + $200D = क्ष् → क्ष्‍
ष + ◌् + $200D = ष् → ष्‍	ळ्ह + ◌् + $200D = ळ्ह् → ळ्ह्‍	ज्ञ + ◌् + $200D = ज्ञ् → ज्ञ्‍
स + ◌् + $200D = स् → स्‍		
ह + ◌् + $200D = ह्		

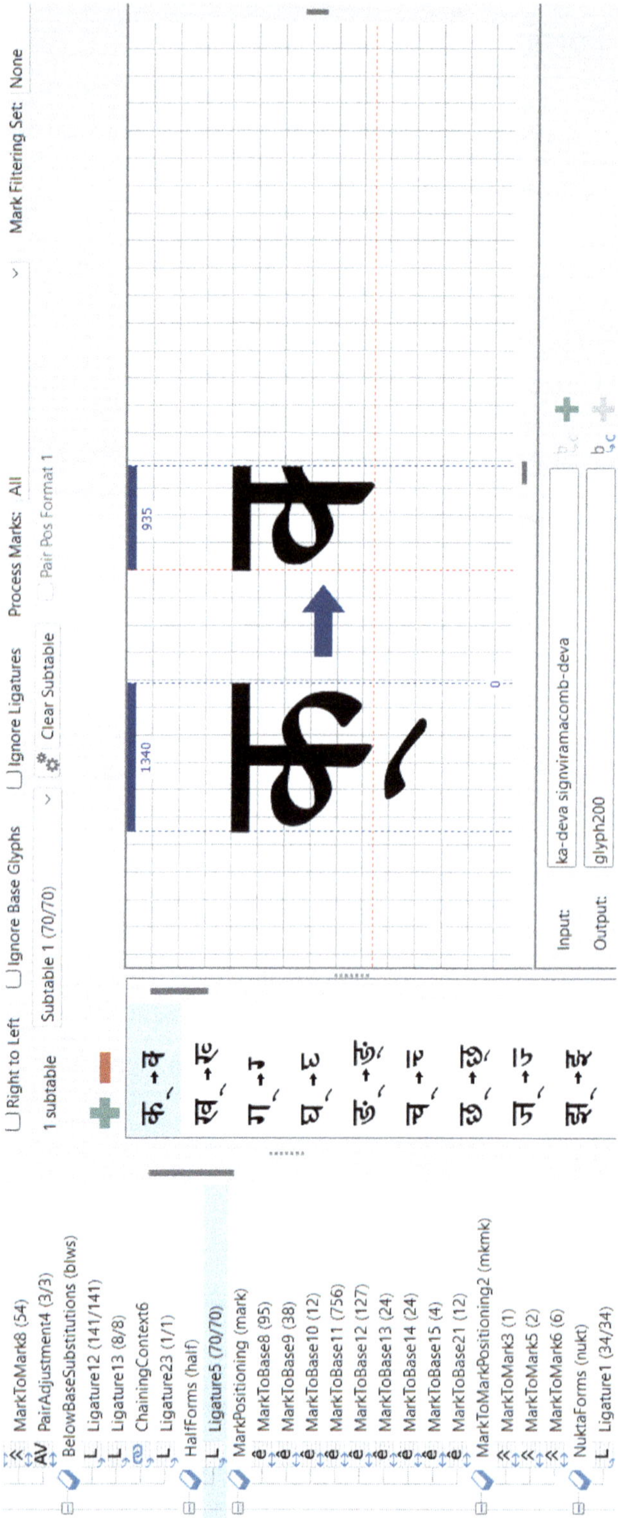
MarkToMark8 (54)
PairAdjustment4 (3/3)
BelowBaseSubstitutions (blws)
Ligature12 (141/141)
Ligature13 (8/8)
ChainingContext6
Ligature23 (1/1)
HalfForms (half)
Ligature5 (70/70)
MarkPositioning (mark)
MarkToBase8 (95)
MarkToBase9 (38)
MarkToBase10 (12)
MarkToBase11 (756)
MarkToBase12 (127)
MarkToBase13 (24)
MarkToBase14 (24)
MarkToBase15 (4)
MarkToBase21 (12)
MarkToMarkPositioning2 (mkmk)
MarkToMark3 (1)
MarkToMark5 (2)
MarkToMark6 (6)
NuktaForms (nukt)
Ligature1 (34/34)
Right to Left
Ignore Base Glyphs
Ignore Ligatures
Process Marks: All
Mark Filtering Set: None
1 subtable
Subtable 1 (70/70)
Clear Subtable
Pair Pos Format 1
1340
935
0
Input: ka-deva signviramacomb-deva
Output: glyph200

Devanāgari Half Forms with Halant

Half Forms customarily with Halant ङ् छ् ट् ठ् ड् ढ् द् ह् uses code HalantForms (haln)

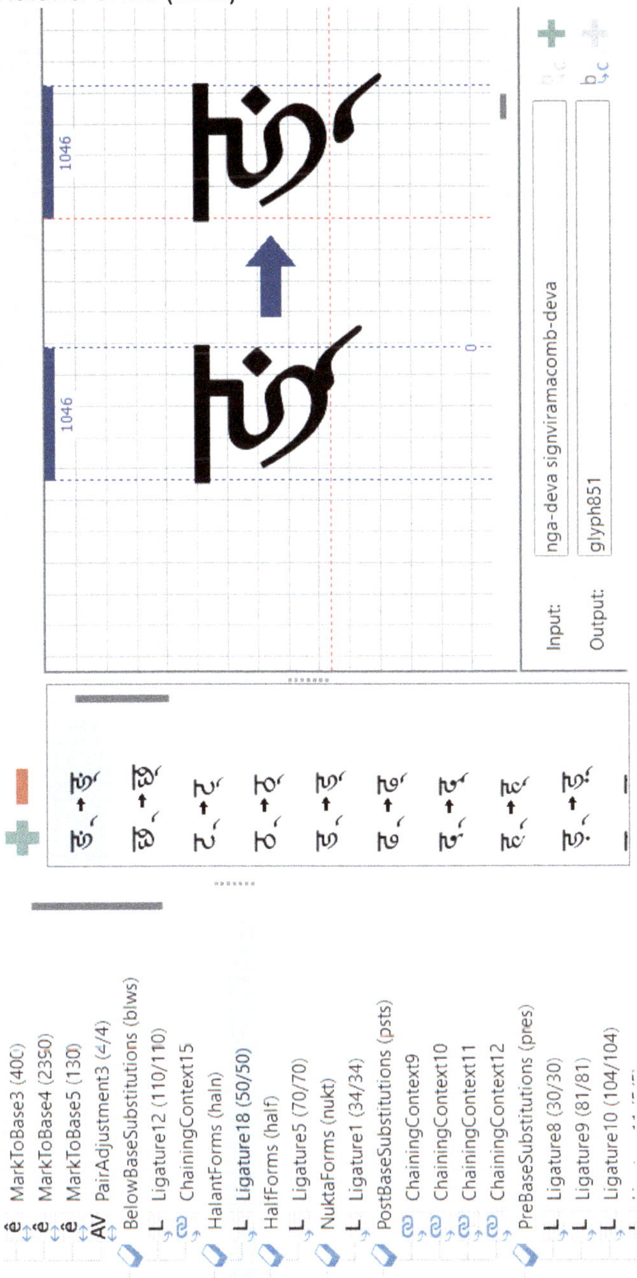

Devanāgari Half Forms for Repha

Repha has its own independent code RephForms (rphf)

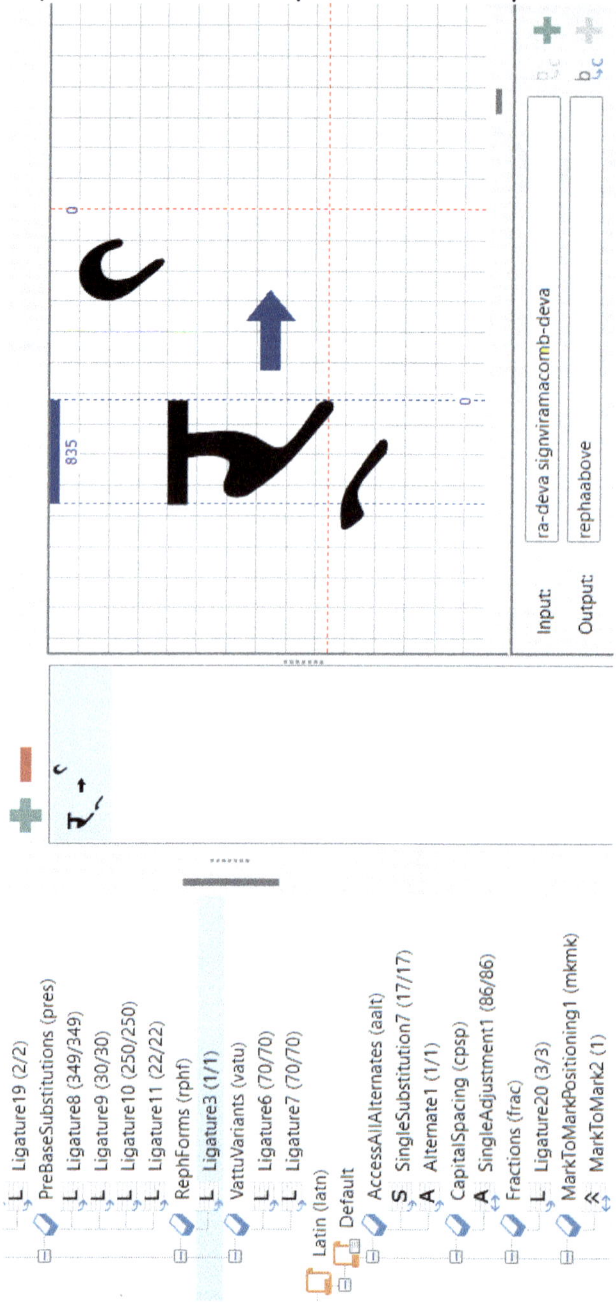

Devanāgari Half Forms needing Implementation

Note: The Vedic character U+097A Devanagari Heavy ya ॺ, has not so far been accounted for by the Indic Shaping Engine code Halfforms (half). Hence it does not allow the Halant ् to get attached while typing on the keyboard.

It has been implemented using BelowBaseSubstitutions (blws).

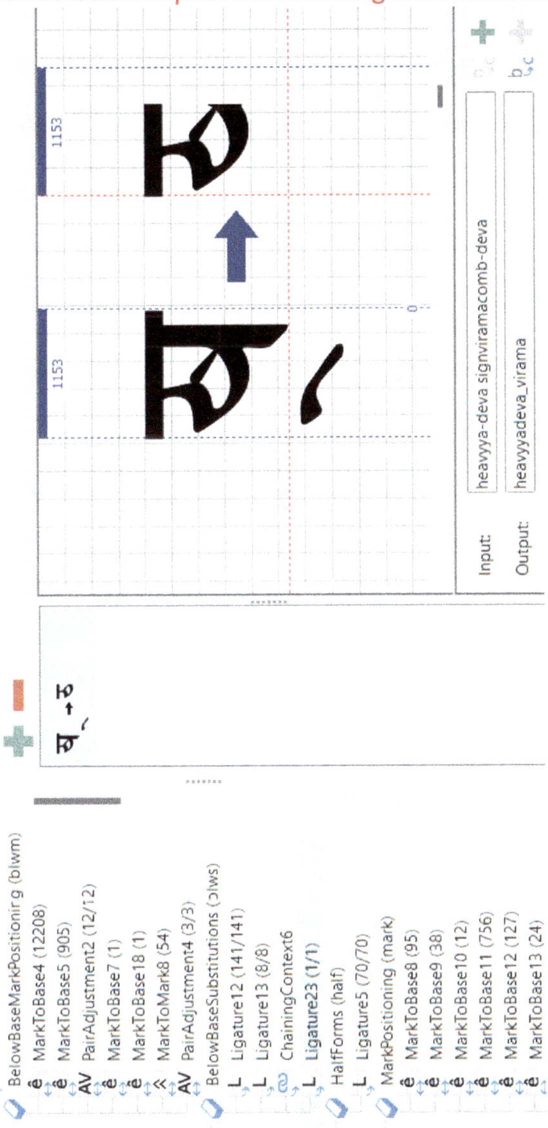

Desirable Conjuncts for clarity and conciseness

A list of desirable ligatures for beautiful Devanagari typesetting that prevents confusion and has clear readability.

स्त्र स्त्र स्त्र

त्त्व त्त्व

ध ध

Ancient Devanāgari Glyphs

In ancient texts some glyphs are seen which have been superseded in recent texts by newer glyphs. This is also known as Allograph.

Ancient / Recent vowels			
अ / अ	आ / आ	ओ / ओ	औ / औ
Ancient / Recent consonants			
झ / झ	ण / ण		
Ancient / Recent conjuncts			
क्ष / क्ष			
Ancient / Recent half-forms			
झ्/झ्	ण् /ण्	क्ष्/क्ष्	
Ancient / Recent numerals			
५ / ५	८ /८	९ / ९	

U+094E ॎ Vowel Sign Prishthamatra represented ॎ while combining		
ॎ + ए → ऐ	ॎ + आ → ओ	ॎ + ओ → औ
U+094E ॱ Sign high spacing dot		

Alternate Glyphs

Sometimes we wish to use an alternate form of a letter or glyph during teaching or for clarity.

श / श	इ / इ	ॐ / ॐ	ध / ध	न / न

Repha रकार

Repha with vowelsign उकार / ऊकार

Customarily ◌ु / ◌ू is used for repha instead of ◌ु / ◌ू

र + ◌ु = रु → रु	र + ◌ू = रू → रू

The code BelowBasesubstitutions (blws) is used.

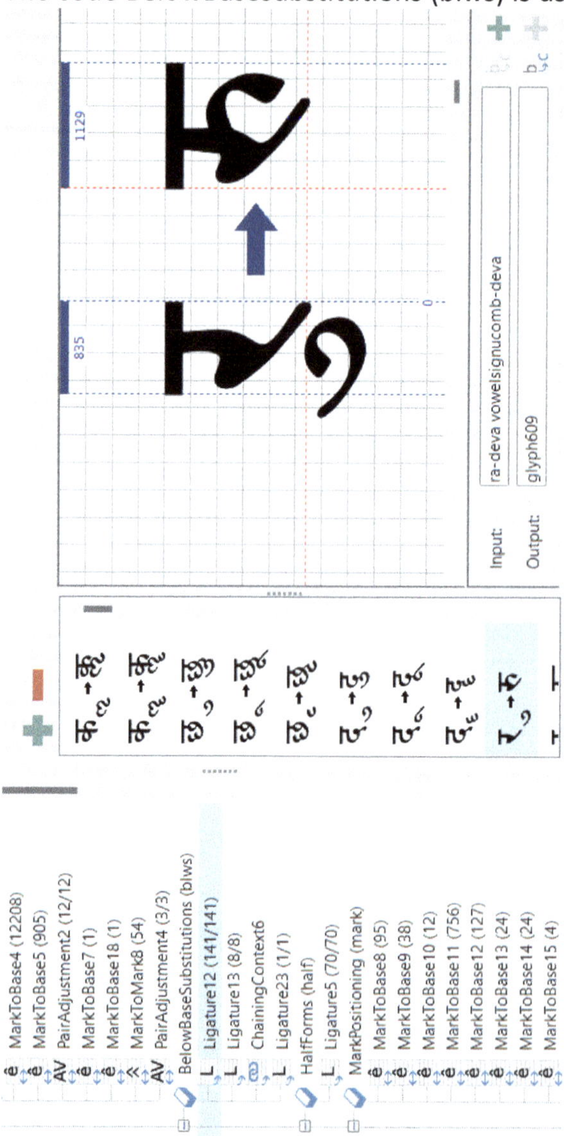

Repha with vowelsign ऋकार / लृकार

Both forms are prevalent रृ / र्ऋ

र + ृ → रृ / र्ऋ	र + ॄ → रॄ / र्ॠ
र + ॢ → रॢ / र्ऌ	र + ॣ → रॣ / र्ॡ

Repha when 2nd letter in Conjunct

In such cases, there are three distinct forms of repha, ◌् र

क + ◌् + र → क्र
ट + ◌् + र → ट्र
र + ◌् + र → र्र

2nd letter Repha as a short slash क्र ख्र ग्र घ्र च्र छ्र ज्र झ्र ञ्र ण्र त्र थ्र द्र ध्र न्र प्र फ्र ब्र भ्र म्र य्र व्र श्र ष्र स्र ह्र I Encoded in two steps, BelowBaseForms (blwf), and then VattuVariants (vatu) in Open Type Design.

2nd letter Repha as a circumflex below ङ्र ट्र ठ्र ड्र ढ्र ल्र ळ्र ष्र I Encoded in single step BelowBaseForms (blwf) in Open Type Design.

2nd letter Repha as Repha र्र I Encoded in single step RephForms (rphf) in Open Type Design.

2nd Repha as a circumflex below र्

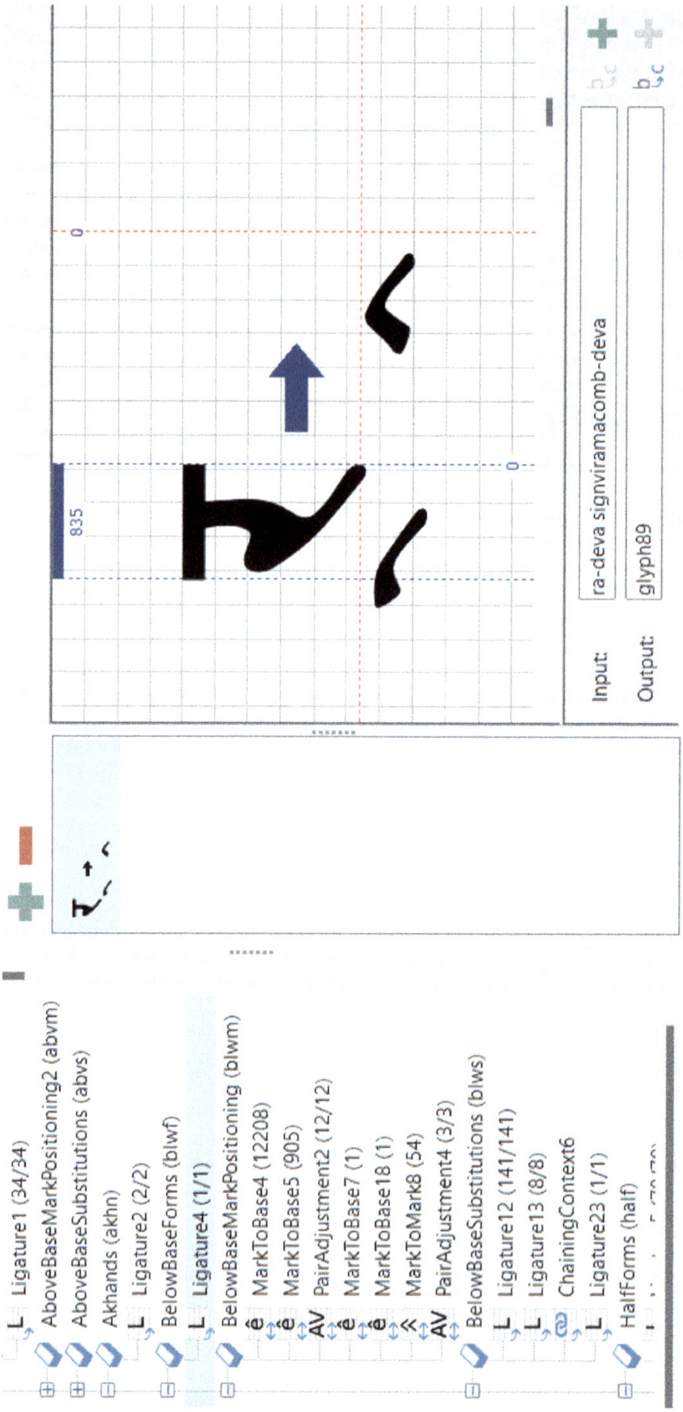

2nd Repha as a short slash क

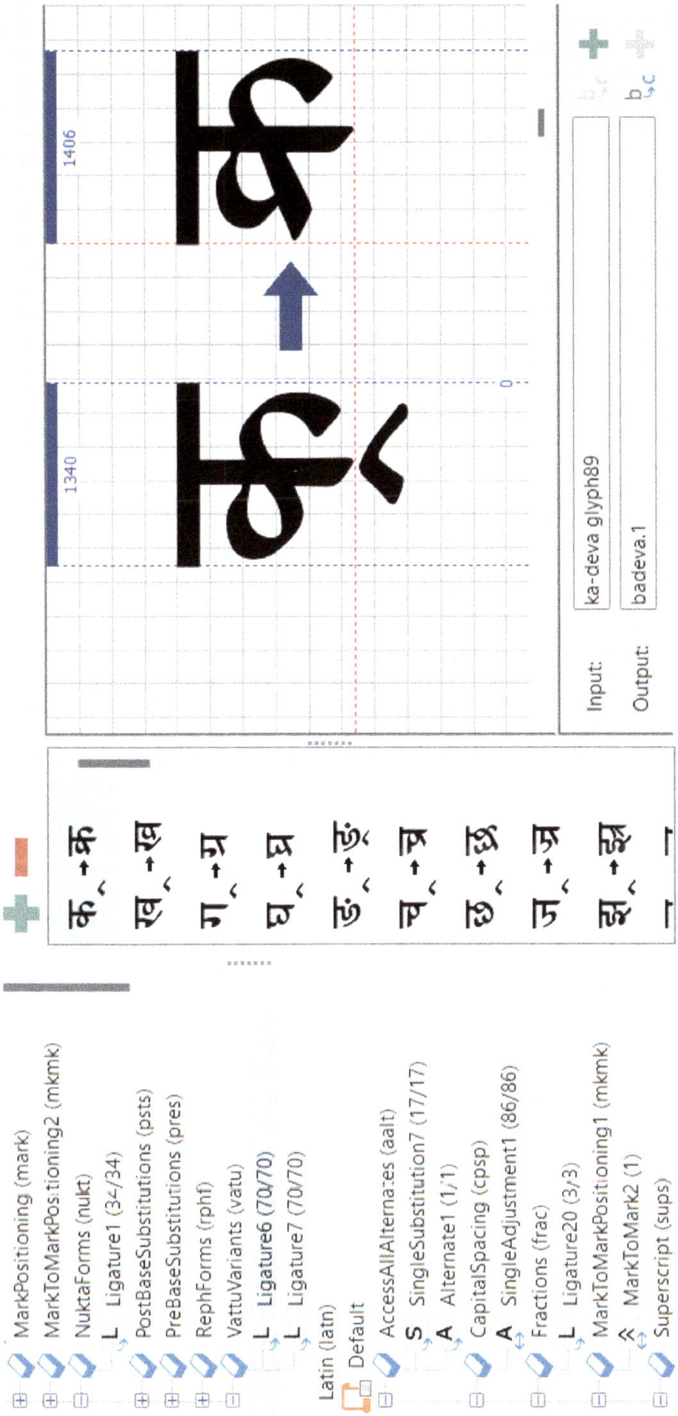

2nd letter Repha as Repha र्

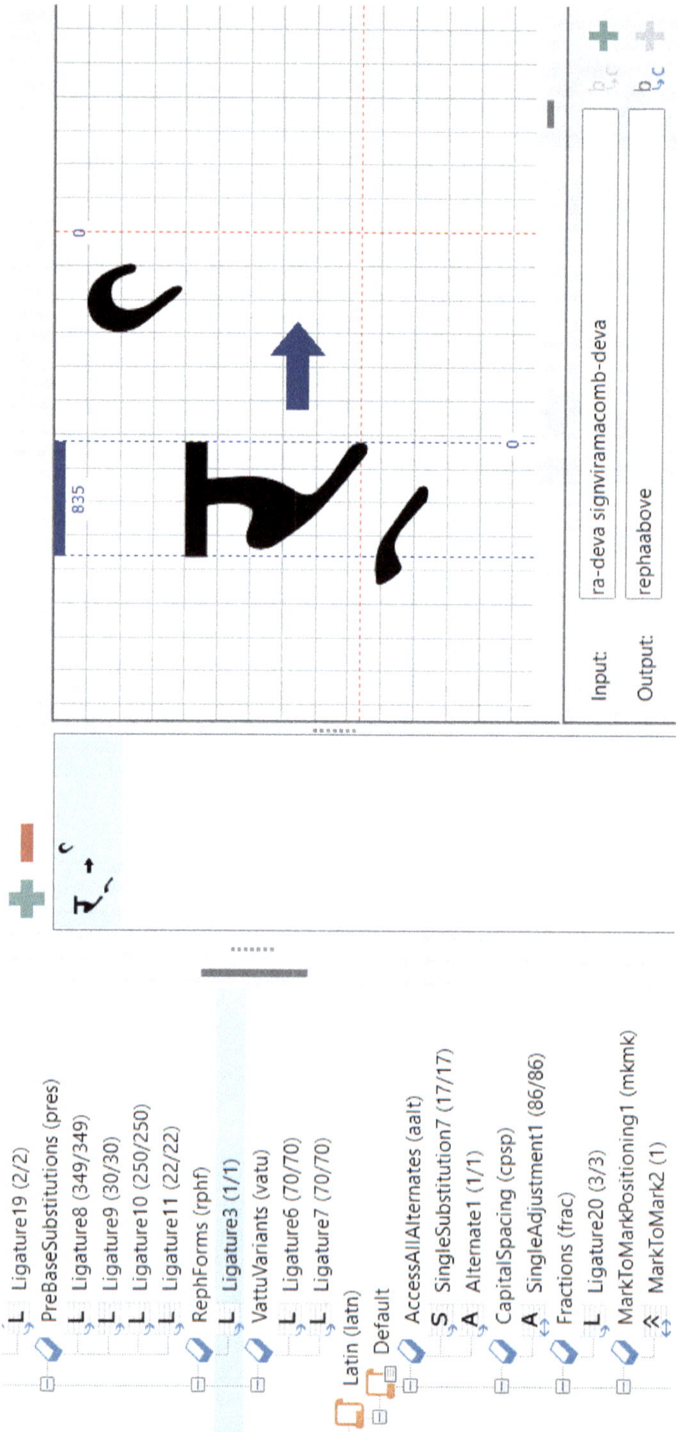

Unicode Character sets for Vedic Sanskrit Font

To design a complete font to serve the purpose of typesetting Vedic Sanskrit texts and classical Sanskrit texts, the Unicode character sets needed are:

- Devanagari U+0900 to 097F (128/128 characters). Some characters here are for languages other than Sanskrit, e.g. Marwari, Dravidian, etc.
- Vedic Extensions U+1CD0 to 1CFF (43/48 characters, last 5 unallocated). All 43 characters are needed.
- Devanagari Extended U+A8E0 to A8FF (32/32 characters). Few characters here are for other languages.

Apart from these, we shall need:

- Basic Latin U+20 to 7E (95/95 characters).
- Latin-1 Supplement U+A0 to BE, F7 (approx 32 characters).
- General Punctuation U+2009 to 203A. (approx 22 characters).
- Currency Symbols U+20A8, 20AC, 20B9 (approx 3 characters).
- Letterlike Symbols U+2122.
- Mathematical Operators U+2212, 2219.
- Geometric Shapes U+25CC.
- Private Use Area U+E000 onwards. For many glyphs, including half-forms, conjunct ligatures, ligatures to support typesetting where Open Type shaping engine is not correctly implemented in Editor or typing software, etc.

Note: For Devanagari to Latin transliteration, many encodings are prevalent, including IAST, Velthius, ISO15919, Harvard-Kyoto, etc. These have relied on Latin Extended-A U+0100 onwards, and Latin Extended Additional U+1E0C onwards. However these are rather incomplete to do Vedic Texts which have many Accents.

We propose a new Unicode block for the same, or collecting all the requisite glyphs in the Private Use Area block.

Devanagari – 0900 to 097F

Characters used in Sanskrit Language, Vedic and Classical.

Vedic Extensions – 1CD0 to 1CFF

Out of 48 characters, 43 characters 1CD0 - 1CFA have been allocated and are in use. The last 5 characters 1CFB - 1CFF are unallocated in Unicode Standard Version 15.0 dated Sept 2022.

Devanagari Extended – A8E0 to A8FF

Out of 32 characters, initial 24 are in fair use in Sanskrit literature. Of the last 8 characters A8F8 – A8FF, some are punctuations seen in ancient texts, and the last two are vowels used in Hindi/Awadhi or other languages.

A8F8	꣸	Sign Pushpika (punctuation/paragraph marker)
A8F9	꣹	Gap Filler (punctuation)
A8FA	꣺	Caret (punctuation to indicate missing letter)
A8FB	ꣻ	Headstroke (Vedic Sanskrit)
A8FC	꣼	Sacred Sign Siddham (Ancient texts)
A8FD	ꣽ	Sacred Jain OM (Jainism texts)
A8FE	ꣾ	Letter AY (languages other than Sanskrit)
A8FF	ꣿ	Vowel Sign AY (languages other than Sanskrit)

Additional Character sets needed

For making a robust and complete Devanagari font for typesetting Classical and Vedic Sanskrit, some additional Unicode character sets are needed. Most of these character sets are needed partially only, except for Basic Latin which is needed in toto for the font to function well.

Basic Latin U+20 to 7E (95/95 characters)

Latin-1 Supplement U+A0 to BE, F7 (approx 32 characters)

Latin Extended-B U+0192

U+0192 ƒ small letter f with hook, used for Windows encoding.

Spacing Modifier Letters U+02BC (approx 4 characters)

U+02BC ʼ U+02C6 ˆ U+02C9 ˉ U+02DC ˜ Used for Windows encoding.

Greek and Coptic $03BC (1 character)

U+03BC μ Greek small letter Mu, used for Windows encoding.

Tibetan U+0FD5, 0FD6 (2 characters)

U+0FD5 ࿕ , U+0FD6 ࿖ svastI = sacred symbols for well-being.

General Punctuation U+2009 to 203A. (approx 22 characters)

Currency Symbols U+20A8, 20AC, 20B9 (approx 3 characters)

U+20A8 ₨ Rupee Sign

U+20AC € Euro Sign

U+20B9 ₹ Indian Rupee Sign

Letterlike Symbols U+2122

U+2122 ™ Trademark

Mathematical Operators U+2212, 2219

U+2212 − minus sign

U+2219 ∙ bulleted list operator

Geometric Shapes U+25CC

U+25CC ◌ dotted circle, used by Indic Shaping software to indicate some mark glyph is missing a base glyph for attachment.

Private Use Area U+E000 onwards

For many glyphs, including half-consonants, special ligatures, conjunct ligatures, ligatures that are a part of typesetting Vedic Sanskrit and are as yet not encoded in Open Type Design Indic Shaping software, etc.

Transliteration Glyphs for Devanāgari to Latin

We use glyphs from various Unicode character sets for efficient transliteration.

One thing to note is that Transliteration is needed to enable non-native readers of Sanskrit Devanagari script to read correctly using Latin transliteration. However this transliteration must NOT jeopardize the pronunciation for native speakers of Sanskrit.

In particular, the transliteration for final 'a' of a word i.e. the final devanagari letter that does not have any vowel sign attached, must be carefully transliterated. Otherwise, the native speakers shall mispronunce it as 'aa', thus distorting the Sanskrit language entirely. In a Devanagari font, a new character that suppresses 'long a' when uttering words having 'a' at end. E.g. Lord Ram vs Rām vs Rāma. One thing is accuracy in transliteration for foreign speakers, however if it changes pronunciation for native speakers, that is a grave anomaly and must be addressed forthwith.

Proposal for Final a = अ

We propose the glyph "ᵃ = U+1D43 Modifier letter small a" that will be used in Latin transliteration for 'final a = अ in a word'.

- राम योग रामायण सूर्य मोह विवेक वैराग्य Vairāgyᵃ
- Character ᵃ, e.g. Rāmᵃ, Yogᵃ, Rāmāyaṇᵃ, Suryᵃ, Mohᵃ, Vivekᵃ

Alternative Transliteration proposals:

- This can be 'a' in extra light font, e.g. Rāma, Yoga
- This can be 'a' in 4 points lower font size, e.g. Rāma, Yoga
- This can be 'a' in gray shade font, e.g. Rāma, Yoga

Perhaps then it shall not elongate the 'a' for native speakers when reading/speaking aloud the text.

Transliteration Glyphs

We see that English has 26 letters of the alphabet, while Sanskrit has 56 letters of the alphabet. Which means we can map only 26 letters directly, and we shall need 30 extra characters for representing the remaining letters of Sanskrit. Hithero people have used Unicode supplement and extended blocks. We propose that the Private Use Area block can be efficiently used while developing a new Sanskrit Font for the same.

English Alphabet 26 letters
a b c d e f g h I j k l m n o p q r s t u v w x y z

Sanskrit Alphabet 56 letters

- 14 vowel letters
  अ आ इ ई उ ऊ ऋ ॠ ऌ ॡ ए ऐ ओ औ
- 3 ayogavaha letters
  ◌ं ◌ः ◌ँ
- 33 consonant letters
  क ख ग घ ङ च छ ज झ ञ ट ठ ड ढ ण त थ द ध न प फ ब भ म य र ल व श
  ष स ह
- 2 Vedic Sanskrit consonant letters
  ळ य
- 1 ardhavisarga
  ◌ᳲ Vedic Sanskrit ayogavaha letter (ideally we must use this same glyph for transliteration from the Vedic Extensions block, instead of finding a new glyph).
- 3 long anusvara
  ꣳ ꣴ ꣴ् Vedic Sanskrit ayogavaha letters (ideally we must use the same glyphs for transliteration from the Vedic Extensions and Devanagari Extended blocks).

Note: Sanskrit has additional symbols for accents, diacritics, etc., those have not been covered in transliteration just yet, as that is not a significant need for any non-native reader for regular texts.

Extra Characters Needed

Extra characters needed apart from Basic Latin Unicode block for Devanagari transliteration.

Note: Transliteration shall follow the English scheme of **caps and no caps**, hence two glyphs per Sanskrit letter.

Sanskrit	Latin Transliteration Character		
Letter	Transliteration with CAPS and no caps		
	IAST	Unicode	ISO 15919
आ	Ā ā	U+0100, U+0101	Ā ā
ई	Ī ī	U+012A, U+012B	Ī ī
ऊ	Ū ū	U+016A, U+016B	Ū ū
ऋ	Ṛ ṛ	U+1E5A, U+1E5B	R̥ r̥ U+0052+0325, U+0072+0325
ॠ	Ṝ ṝ	U+1E5C, U+1E5D	R̥̄ r̥̄ U+0052+0325+0304, U+0072+0325+0304
ऌ	Ḷ ḷ	U+1E36, U+1E37	L̥ l̥ U+004C+0325, U+006C+0325
ॡ	Ḹ ḹ	U+1E38, U+1E39	L̥̄ l̥̄ U+004C+0325+0304, U+006C+0325+0304
ए	E e	U+0045, U+0065	Ē ē U+112, U+113
ओ	O o	U+004F, U+006F	Ō ō U+014C, U+014D
Existing transliteration schemes have two letters for each of these, we have proposed a single new letter			
ऐ	AI ai	U+0041+0049, U+0061+0069	AI ai
औ	AU au	U+0041+0055, U+0061+0075	AU au
ऐ	Æ æ	U+00C6, U+00E6	Proposed
औ	Œ œ	U+0152, U+0153	Proposed
Perhaps no caps is needed here since no word begins with it – an ayogavaha letter coming at the end of a word, however CAPS is given for Uniformity during teaching			
◌ं	Ṃ ṃ	U+1E42, U+1E43	Ṁ ṁ U+1E40, U+1E41

◌ः	Ḥ ḥ	U+1E24, U+1E25	Ḥ ḥ
◌ँ	~	U+0303 e.g. ॐ OM̃ om̃	M̐ m̐ U+004D+0310, U+006D+0310 e.g. ॐ ŌM̐ ōm̐
ऽ	'	U+0027	'
Vedic Letters			
ळ	Ḻ ḻ	U+1E3A, U+1E3B	Ḷ ḷ U+1E36, U+1E37
य़	NA		Y̌ y̌ U+0059+030C, U+0079+030C
◌ᳵ	NA		H̱ ẖ U+0048+0331,U+0068+0331
◌ᳶ	Propose ◌ᳶ the same glyph for transliteration		
ꣲ ꣳ ꣴ	Propose ꣲ ꣳ ꣴ the same glyphs for transliteration		

Note:
ISO 15919 can be encoded using the Unicode Blocks

- Basic Latin and Combining Diacritical Marks

or we may use the Unicode Blocks

- Latin Extended-A and Latin Extended Additional

The encoding for Avagraha ऽ is ' U+0027 = apostrophe character. It is not the character given on standard laptop keyboards ‘ U+2018 = Left single quotation mark.

IAST

International Alphabet of Sanskrit Transliteration (IAST)

	0101		012B		016B	1E5B	1E5D	1E37	1E39
a	ā	i	ī	u	ū	ṛ	ṝ	ḷ	ḹ
अ	आ	इ	ई	उ	ऊ	ऋ	ॠ	ऌ	ॡ
				1E43	0303	1E25	NA	1E43	
e	ai	o	au	ṃ	˜	ḥ	Ardha Visarga	oṃ / om̐	
ए	ऐ	ओ	औ	◌ं	◌ँ	◌ः	◌ᳲ	ॐ	
Consonants shown with vowel 'a = अ' for uttering									
ka	क	ca	च	ṭa	ट	ta	त	pa	प
kha	ख	cha	छ	ṭha	ठ	tha	थ	pha	फ
ga	ग	ja	ज	ḍa	ड	da	द	ba	ब
gha	घ	jha	झ	ḍha	ढ	dha	ध	bha	भ
ṅa	ङ	ña	ञ	ṇa	ण	na	न	ma	म
ya	ra	la	va		śa	ṣa	sa	ha	
य	र	ल	व		श	ष	स	ह	
NA = Not Available as not currently IAST encoded. We use ISO 15919									
1E3B	0027	y̌	h̲		Note: Consonant only				
ḻa	'	NA	NA		ka	क्अ = क			
ळ	ऽ	य	◌ᳲ		k	क्			

ISO 15919 uses some combining characters

r̥ = r + U0325 ring below	r̥̄ = r + U0325 + U0304 macron above	l̥ = l + U0325 ̥ ring below	l̥̄ = l + U0325 + U304 macron above
m̐ = m + U0310 ̐candrabindu above			
y̌ = y + U030C ̌ caron above		h̲ = h + U0331 _ macron below or U+1E96	

ISO 15919

International Standards Organisation for Devanagari Transliteration

	0101		012B		016B	0325	0304	0325	0304
a	ā	i	ī	u	ū	r̥	r̥̄	l̥	l̥̄
अ	आ	इ	ई	उ	ऊ	ऋ	ॠ	ऌ	ॡ
0113		014D		1E41	0310	1E25	1E96	1E41	
ē	ai	ō	au	ṁ	m̐	ḥ	ẖ	oṁ / om̐	
ए	ऐ	ओ	औ	◌ं	◌ँ	◌ः	◌ᳵ	ॐ	
Consonants shown with vowel 'a = अ' for uttering									
				1E45					00F1
ka	kha	ga	gha	ṅa	ca	cha	ja	jha	ña
क	ख	ग	घ	ङ	च	छ	ज	झ	ञ
1E6D		1E0D		1E47					
ṭa	ṭha	ḍa	ḍha	ṇa	ta	tha	da	dha	na
ट	ठ	ड	ढ	ण	त	थ	द	ध	न
pa	pha	ba	bha	ma					
प	फ	ब	भ	म					
					015B	1E63			
ya	ra	la	va		śa	ṣa	sa	ha	
य	र	ल	व		श	ष	स	ह	
1E37	0027	030C	1E96		Note: Consonant only				
ḷa	'	y̌	ẖ		ka	क्अ = क			
ळ	ऽ	य़	◌ᳵ		k	क्			

Note: Unicode is given for uncommon letters. (keyboard ALT+X).
ISO 15919 uses Combining Diacritical Marks, but Latin Extended may be used alternatively. E.g. ē = U+0065+0304 or ē = U+0113

IAST and ISO 15919 Differences in encoding characters

IAST

1E43	0303	1E43	1E3B			1E5B	1E5D	1E37	1E39
ṃ	˜	oṃ	ḻa	NA	NA	ṛ	ṝ	ḷ	ḹ
ं	ँ	ॐ	ळ	य़	◌ᳵ	ऋ	ॠ	ऌ	ॡ

ISO 15919

1E41	0310	1E41	1E37	030C	1E96	0325	0325 +0304	0325	0325 +0304
ṁ	m̐	ṁ	ḷa	y̌	ẖ	r̥	r̥̄	l̥	l̥̄
ं	ँ	ॐ	ळ	य	◌ᳵ	ऋ	ॠ	ऌ	ॡ

Sanskrit	IAST	Unicode	ISO 15919	Unicode
ए	e	U+0065	ē	U+113
ओ	o	U+006F	ō	U+014D

Unicode Blocks used by IAST and ISO 15919

Some characters from the Supplement and Extended blocks are used by the transliteration schemes. These Unicode blocks are:

Latin-1 Supplement – A0 to FF

Latin Extended A – 0100 to 017F

Latin Extended Additional – 1E00 to 1EFF

Then we have the Combining Diacritical Marks block, most of these characters cannot be typed directly from the keyboard, rather we need to use Insert-Symbol-More Symbols and choose the font and the subset, find the requisite character and insert it.

Combining Diacritical Marks – 0300 to 036F

IAST and ISO 15919 Devanagari to Latin Transliteration characters

Unicode	Symbol	Meaning	Remarks
0027	'	Apostrophe	ऽ avagraha
Note: Keyboards have U+2018 ‘ Left single quotation mark			
0303	˜	Combining tilde above	om̃ IAST
Note: Keyboards have U+007E ~ Tilde			
0304	¯	Combining macro above	ē
0307	˙	Combining dot above	anusvara
030C	ˇ	Combining caron above	y̌ ISO 15919
030D	ˈ	Combining vertical line above	Vedic svarita
030E	ˮ	Combining double vertical line above	Vedic dirgha svarita
U+030D and U+030E are not used in Transliteration, rather they may be used to type Vedic Sanskrit in absence of Vedic Extensions block			
0310	̐	Combining candrabindu above	candrabindu
0323	.	Combining dot below	ṃ
0325	˳	Combining ring below	r̥ ISO 15919
0331	ˍ	Combining macron below	ḻ IAST

Redundant Glyphs earlier used for Transliteration

U+0953 Devanagari grave accent ॓

U+0954 Devanagari acute accent ॔

These glyphs are no longer in use since they do not have Indic shaping properties in Open Type design code. Just present to maintain continuity with earlier versions of Unicode when Sanskrit to Latin transliteration used these symbols. These are now superseded by symbols U+0300 ̀ Combining grave accent, U+0301 ́ Combining acute accent. However, even these symbols are not seen in transliteration.

Devanāgari Glyphs in a Sanskrit Font

Open Type design that uses Indic shaping engine rules exhibits the given features. Only the glyphs used for Sanskrit Language typesetting are listed. (The Devanagari script is used to write many languages, not all glyphs are used by Sanskrit).

Repha Conjunct Glyphs

For the Repha, conjunct glyphs vary as per previous or next letter.

- Repha as 1st letter in a conjunct, Repha half consonant र्= र्
  e.g. RephaKakara conjunct र्क र्ख र्ग etc.
- Repha as 2nd letter in a conjunct ्र, e.g. KakaraRepha क्+र = क्र, similarly ख्र ग्र घ्र ह्र etc.
- Repha as 2nd letter in a conjunct , e.g. ttakaraRepha ट्+र = ट्र, similarly ठ्र, ड्र, ङ्र etc.
- Language other than Sanskrit, e.g. Marathi Repha half consonant र्= ऱ्

Use of Zero width Joiner Glyphs

General Punctuation Unicode Block characters in a Sanskrti font.
U+200C Zero width non-joiner
U+200D Zero width joiner

क्+U+200C +त=क्‌त

क्+U+200D +त=क्‍त

क्+U+200C +ष=क्‌ष

क्+U+200D +ष=क्ष

Use of Dotted Circle Glyph

Geometric Shapes Unicode block Dotted Circle character in a Sanskrti font. It is used by the Indic shaping engine that uses the Devanagari script. (dev/deva).

U+25CC ◌ Dotted Circle

- This is used to indicate the presence of a dependent glyph, that is missing its base glyph for getting attached. ◌ं vs कं
- It is used to type a dependent glyph ◌ा during teaching, etc.

Devanāgari Atomic Consonants

The glyphs that are directly encoded in Unicode table are referred to as atomic glyphs, as they are directly typed without any adjustment or additional glyph. Note: These consonants have the inherent अ vowel.

Classical and Vedic Sanskrit Consonants.
कखगघङ,चछजझञ,टठडढण,तथदधन,पफबभम,यरलव,शषस,ह
Vedic Sanskrit Consonants ळ य

(Consonants with Nukta are used in other languages, Hindi, etc. क़ ख़ ग़ ज़ ड़ ढ़ ऩ फ़ य़)

Devanāgari Vowels

Vowels used in Sanskrit are:
अआ इई उऊ ऋॠ ऌॡ एऐ ओऔ।

Devanāgari Matras (dependent vowel glyphs)

Matras are standard for most consonants.
◌ा ◌ि ◌ी ◌ु ◌ू ◌ृ ◌ॄ ◌ॢ ◌ॣ ◌े ◌ै ◌ो ◌ौ

For the Repha र, there is a change in attaching the vowel matras ◌ु ◌ू ◌ृ ◌ॄ ◌ॢ ◌ॣ।

Devanāgari Halant for Half Form of Consonant

Halant ् (dependent glyph) depicts half-form of a consonant.

क् ख् ग् घ् ङ् च् छ् ज् झ् ञ् ट् ठ् ड् ढ् ण् त् थ् द् ध् न् प् फ् ब् भ् म् य् र् ल् व् श् ष् स् ह्

Devanāgari Anusvara and Visarga (dependent glyphs)

Anusvara ं and Visarga ः are ayogavaha sounds that appear during speaking.

Devanāgari Digits

0 to 9.

० १ २ ३ ४ ५ ६ ७ ८ ९

Devanāgari Punctuation marks

बुद्धियुक्तो जहातीह , उभे सुकृतदुष्कृते । तस्माद् योगाय युज्यस्व , योगः कर्मसु कौशलम् ॥
Bhagavad Gita 2.50

Danda । represents virama = stop. (for a partial verse).

Double danda ॥ represents purna virama = fullstop. (end of a complete verse).

Abbreviation sign ॰ represents an abbreviated word. अष्टाध्यायी । अष्टा॰

Additionally, in typesetting texts in the modern era, the Latin punctuation marks are freely used, e.g. , comma, . full stop, ? question mark, - hyphen, etc.

Devanagari Special Symbols

Om ॐ sacred symbol, used at the beginning of any text.

Avagraha ऽ used in Sanskrit Grammar Sandhi to indicate अ dropped.

प्रथमः अध्यायः । प्रथमोऽध्यायः ।

Rupee symbol ₹ Indian currency (Unicode Currency block). ₹२१०० = Rs 2100.

Svasti 卐 卍 indicates well-being for the reader, is typed at the end of a text (Unicode Tibetan block). 卐 इति 卐

Devanagari other Language specific Letters

We see that a Sanskrit Devangari font needs the Devanagari Unicode block, not all its characters are used by the Sanskrit language.

Devanagari Hindi/Awadhi language specific Letters

U+0904 ऄ vowel , U+090D ऍ vowel , U+090E ऎ vowel

U+0911 ऑ vowel , U+0912 ऒ vowel

U+093C ़ nukta sign

U+0945 candra ॅ (for omkara) ऍ ऎ ऑ ऒ

Devanagari Hindi/Dravidian language specific Letters

U+0929 ऩ nukta consonant, U+0931 ऱ nukta consonant

Devanagari Marathi language specific Letters

U+0933 ळ Also seen in Vedic Sanskrit.

U+0934 ऴ letter with nukta, Marathi/Dravidian.

U+0972 ॲ Candra अ

U+093C ़ nukta sign

Devanagari Marwari language specific Letters

U+0978 ॸ Devanagari Letter Marwari DDA

Devanagari Sindhi language specific Letters
U+097B ॻ , U+097C ॼ , U+097E ॾ, U+097F ॿ

Devanagari Limbu language specific Letters
U+097D ॽ Devanagari Letter Glottal Stop

Devanagari Konkani language specific Letters

Devanagari Bodo Dogri Maithili languages specific Letters
Latin U+02BC modified apostrophe, 093D avagraha

Devanagari Kashmiri and Bihari languages specific
U+093A ◌ऺ, U+093B ◌ऻ vowel signs

U+094F ◌ॏ

U+0973 ॳ Letter oe, U+0974 ॴ Letter ooe

U+0975 ॵ Letter Candra AW

Devanagari Kashmiri language specific Mātrās
U+093A ◌ऺ, U+093B ◌ऻ, U+094F ◌ॏ Vowel Sign
U+0956, U+0957,
U+0976 ॶ, U+ 0977 ॷ

Devanagari Avestan language specific Letters
U+0955 ◌ॕ Vowel Sign

U+0979 ॹ Letter ZHA

Devanagari Sharada Lipi specific Letters
U+0900 ◌ऀ Devanagari Sign inverted Candrabindu

Devanagari pristhmatra Mātrā (a historic glyph)
U+094E ◌ॎ

Keyboard map for Vedic Sanskrit Typing

Normal Keyboard

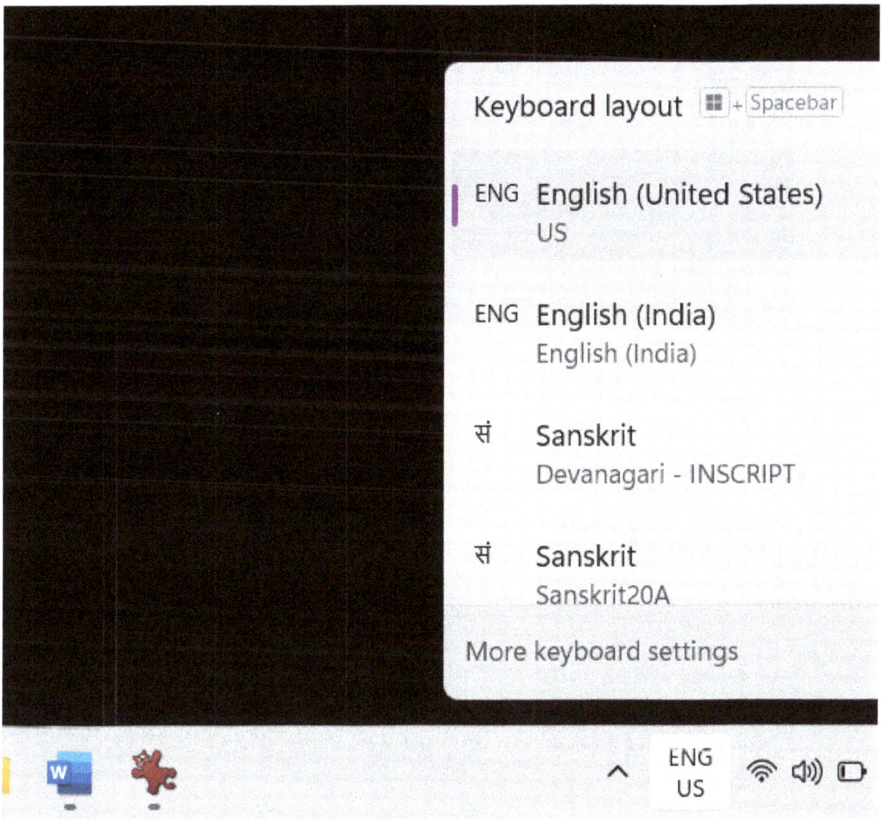

We can download this keyboard map installer file "KbdEditInstallerSANSKRIT2020A.exe" for Windows from https://sourceforge.net/projects/advaita-sharada-font/files/Devanagari/

Unicode Block = Devanagari 0900 to 097F

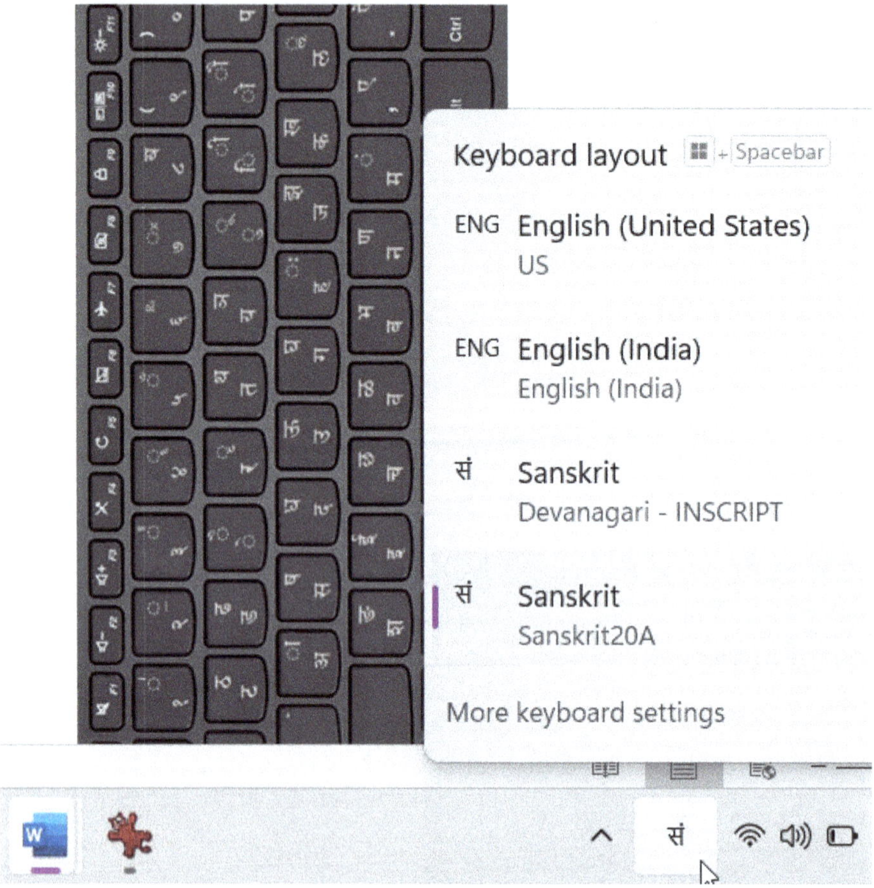

Keyboard with Language Sanskrit selected in Language bar

Use it with and without **SHIFT** key for full access to those Devanagari Unicode Block glyphs needed for Sanskrit language.

A bigger image for clarity is also given.

Unicode Block = Vedic Extensions 1CD0 to 1CFF

Keyboard with Language Sanskrit in Language bar with **PrtSc** Pressed

A bigger image for clarity is also given.

Esc
PrtSc
Insert
Delete
Backspace
Num Lock
Tab
Home
PgUp
Enter
CapsLk
End
PgDn
Shift
Ctrl
Fn
Alt
Ins
Del

Unicode Block = Devanagari Extended A8E0 to A8FF

Keyboard with Language Sanskrit in Language bar with **PrtSc** Pressed. Then with **SHIFT** key press.

A bigger image for clarity is also given.

Esc
F1
F2
F3
F4
F5
F6
F7
F8
F9
F10
F11
F12
PrtSc
Insert
Delete
Backspace
Num Lock
Tab
CapsLk
Enter
Shift
Ctrl
Fn
Alt
Alt
Ctrl
PgUp
PgDn
Home
End
Ins
Del
Shift
Enter

Open Type Design Considerations

Indic Script Devanagari

Select the Script Devanagari (deva) and Latin (latn).
Since script deva is deprecated, we may select script dev2.

See the Shaper(s) required from an existing font.

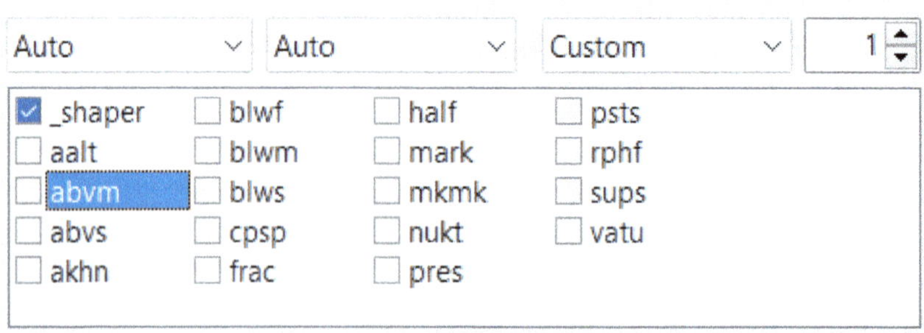

Indic Shaping Features

Add the Shaping Feature(s) required one by one.
There are two principal features in Open Type design, namely Glyph Positioning (GPOS) and Glyph Substitution (GSUB). Each feature has some shaping code lookups, which we can add during Font Design.

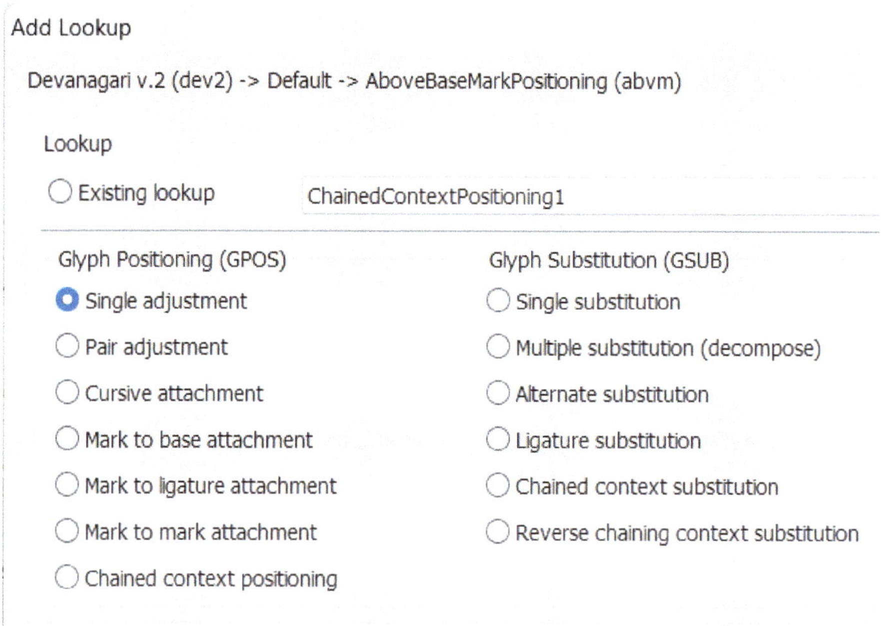

AboveBaseMarkPositioning (abvm)

MarkToBase-attaching anchor of mark glyph with base glyph, e.g. U0915+0902 क ं precise positioning of Mark.

AboveBaseSubstitutions (abvs)

Ligature-replacing overlapping glyphs with new drawn ligature glyphs र्ी र्ीं that do not overlap.

Akhands (akhn)

Ligature-replacing क + ् + ष combination glyphs with new drawn ligature क्ष glyph

BelowBaseForms (blwf)

ChainingContext- क ृ → कृ

BelowBaseMarkPositioning (blwm)

MarkToBase-attaching anchor of mark glyph with base glyph
MarkToMark-attaching anchor of mark glyph with mark glyph

BelowBaseSubstitutions (blws)
Ligature-replacing overlapping glyphs with new drawn smaller glyphs that do not overlap.

ConjunctForms (cjct)
Ligature-replacing consonant glyph combinations, with new drawn ligature glyph, as seen in Sanskrit literature.

HalantForms (haln)
Ligature-replacing glyphs where halant intersects, with new drawn glyph where halant is well positioned.

HalfForms (half)
Ligature-replacing consonant+halant glyphs with new drawn half-consonant glyph.

NuktaForms (nukt)
Ligature-replacing the combination of consonant+nukta glyphs with a new ligature.

PostBaseSubstitutions (psts)
Ligature-replacing the combination of consonant+halant glyphs with a new ligature.

PreBaseSubstitutions (pres)
Ligature-replacing the combination of consonant+halant+consonant glyphs with a new ligature.

RakarForms (rkrf)
Ligature-replacing consonant+halant+repha combination glyphs with new drawn Ligature conjunct having back slash for repha

RephForms (rphf)
Ligature-for replacing repha+halant glyphs with top curve glyph

VattuVariants (vatu)
Ligature-replacing consonant+halant+repha combination glyphs with new Ligature conjunct with caret below for repha

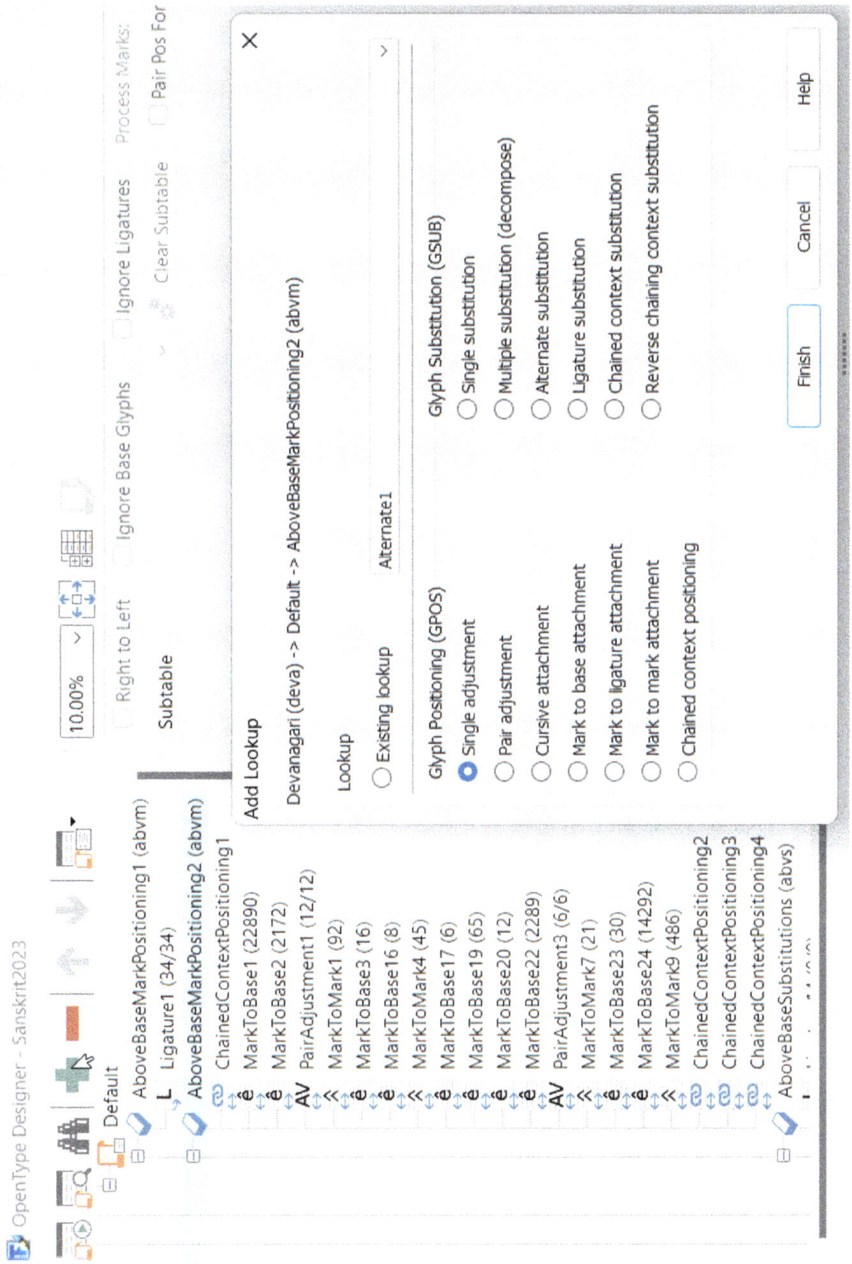

Adding a Feature for the Shaping Engine.

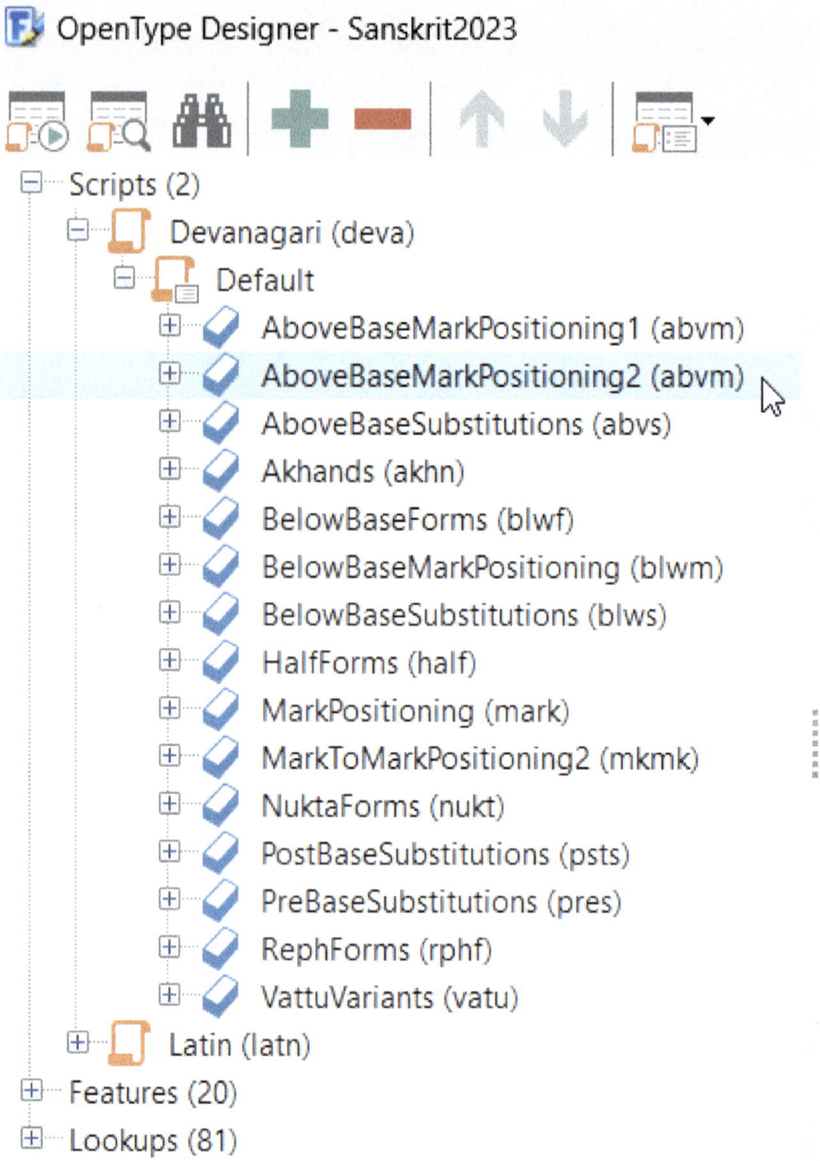

Principal Features needed for a Devanagari Font.

AboveBaseMarkPositioning (abvm)

Feature = MarkToBase
MarkToBase - Attaching anchor of such a mark glyph that must be attached above the base glyph. This works for **two independent glyphs**, and is used to adjust the relative position of both such that the final glyph is correct as per the Sanskrit literature.

It uses Anchors that shall be adjusted for positioning. One glyph has attribute **base glyph**, and the other glyph has attribute **mark glyph**. Then we use the **MarkToBase** feature.

Used for attaching marks like Anusvara, Candrabindu, Svarita (Udatta) to the Vowels and Consonants-with-inherent-vowel.

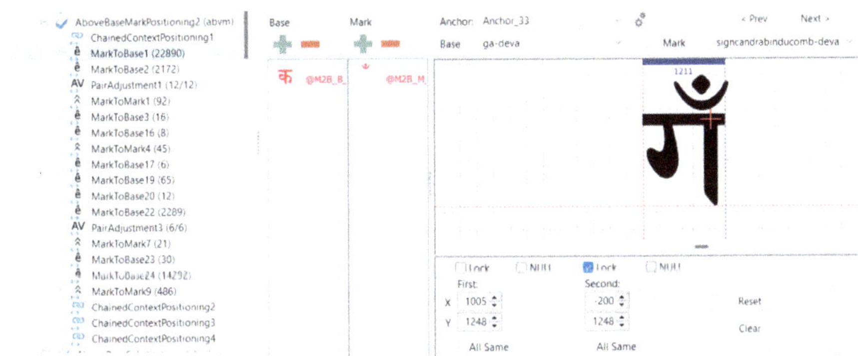

Above mark glyphs array ◌ँ ◌ं ◌॓ ◌॔ ◌॑ Devanagari Block.

Above mark glyphs array ◌᳚ ◌᳛ ◌᳐ ◌̆ ◌᳴ ◌᳸ VedicExtensions Block.

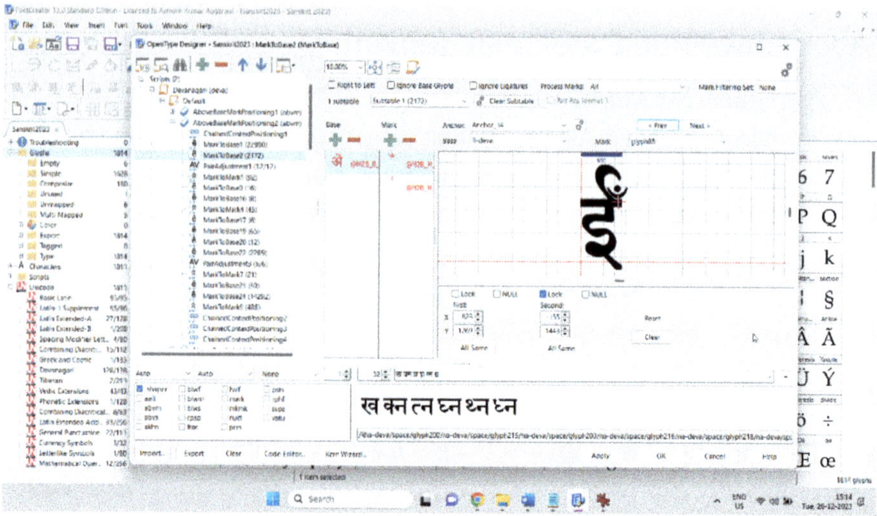

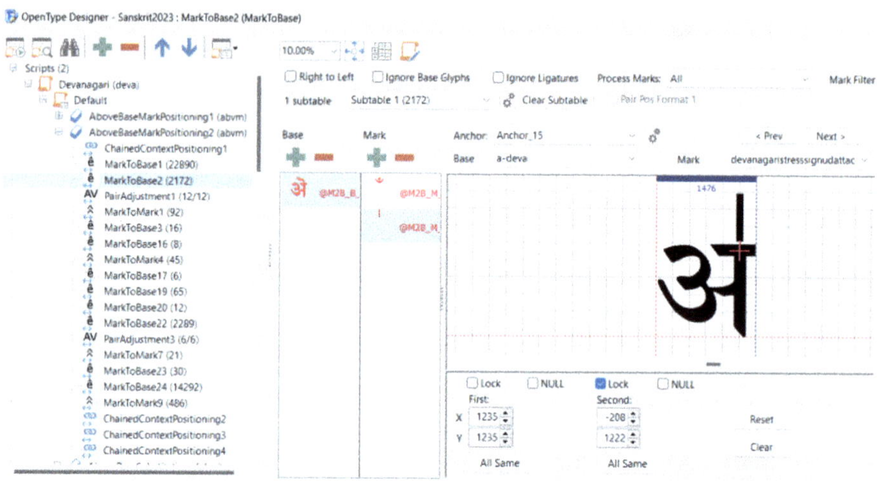

OpenType Designer - Sanskrit2023 : MarkToBase2 (MarkToBase)
Scripts (2)
Devanagari (deva)
Default
AboveBaseMarkPositioning1 (abvm)
AboveBaseMarkPositioning2 (abvm)
ChainedContextPositioning1
MarkToBase1 (22890)
MarkToBase2 (2172)
PairAdjustment1 (12/12)
MarkToMark1 (92)
MarkToBase3 (16)
MarkToBase16 (8)
MarkToMark4 (45)
MarkToBase17 (6)
MarkToBase19 (65)
MarkToBase20 (12)
MarkToBase22 (2289)
PairAdjustment3 (6/6)
MarkToMark7 (21)
MarkToBase23 (30)
MarkToBase24 (14292)
MarkToMark9 (486)
ChainedContextPositioning2
ChainedContextPositioning3
ChainedContextPositioning4
Right to Left
Ignore Base Glyphs
Ignore Ligatures
Process Marks: All
Mark Filter
1 subtable
Subtable 1 (2172)
Clear Subtable
Pair Pos Format 1
Base
Mark
Anchor: Anchor_15
< Prev
Next >
Base a-deva
Mark devanagaristresssignudattac
Lock
NULL
First:
Second:
X 1235
Y 1235
-208
1222
All Same
Reset
Clear

Firstly, we need to specify the dotted circle glyph for all above base marks, that should be inserted in case a required base glyph is absent.

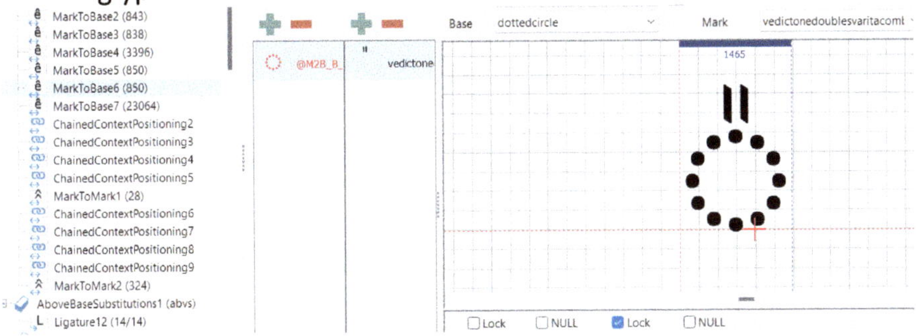

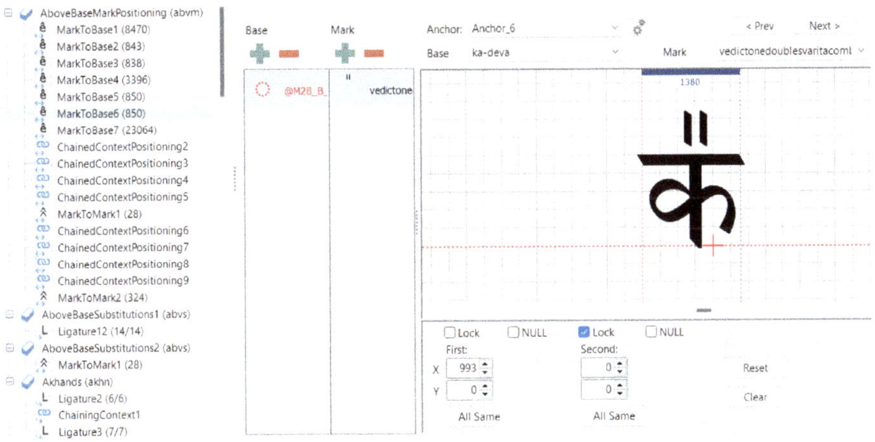

Feature = PairAdjustment

PairAdjustment – Adjusting the precise position of two mark glyphs wrt each other.

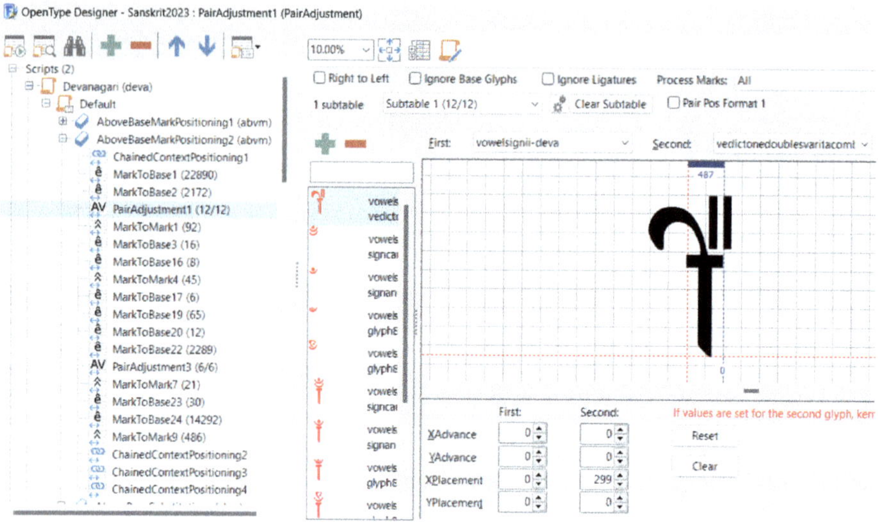

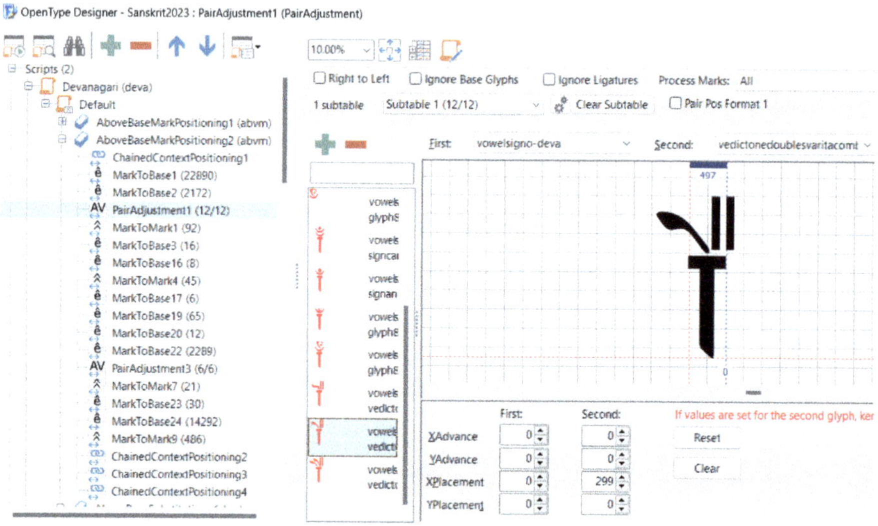

Question: Should we use MarkToMark here?

What actually works? MarkToMark or PairAdjustment?

The fonts SanskritText and AdobeDevanagari do not use PairAdjustment feature here. MarkToMark is used.

Feature = MarkToMark

MarkToMark – Adjusting the precise position of two mark glyphs wrt each other.

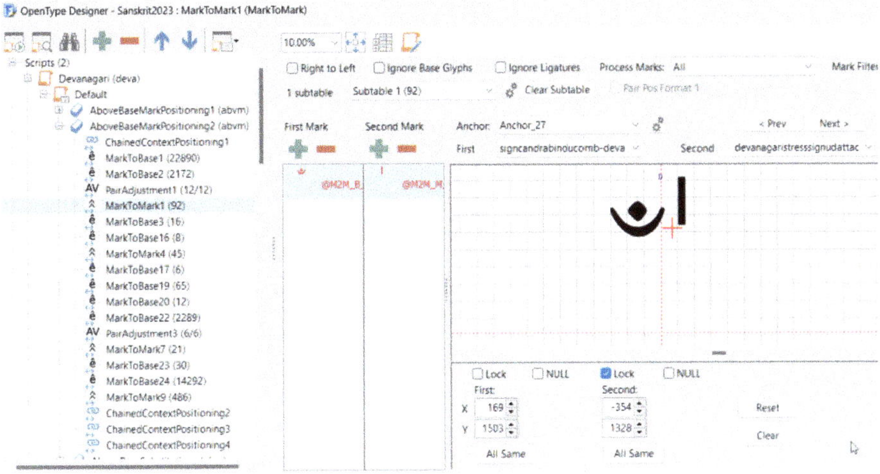

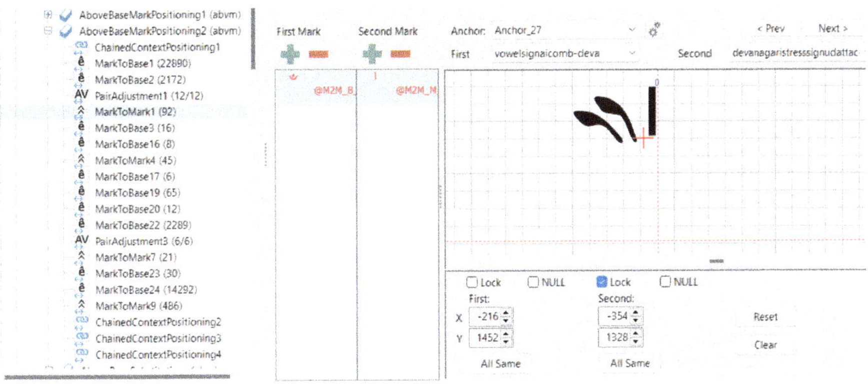

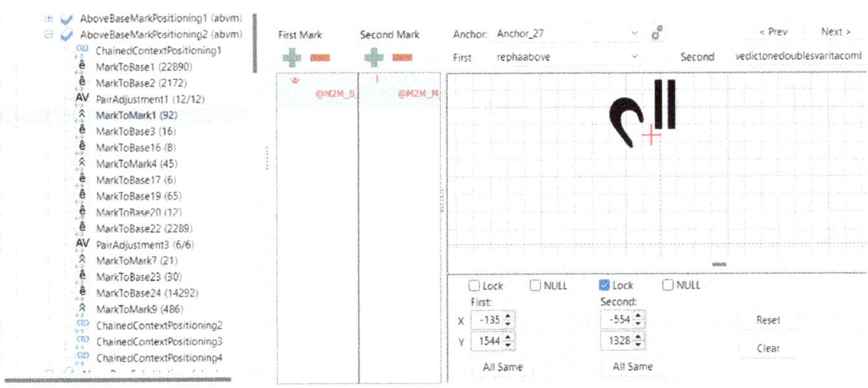

Feature = MarkToBase

MarkToBase – Adjusting the precise position of

- Visarga and Svarita क॑ः
- Visarga and Anudatta क॒ः
- Ardhavisarga and Svarita क॑ᳲ
- Ardhavisarga and Anudatta क॒ᳲ

wrt each other. This helps to position the Svarita to the top of the Letter and not above Visarga. Similarly Anudatta below Letter.

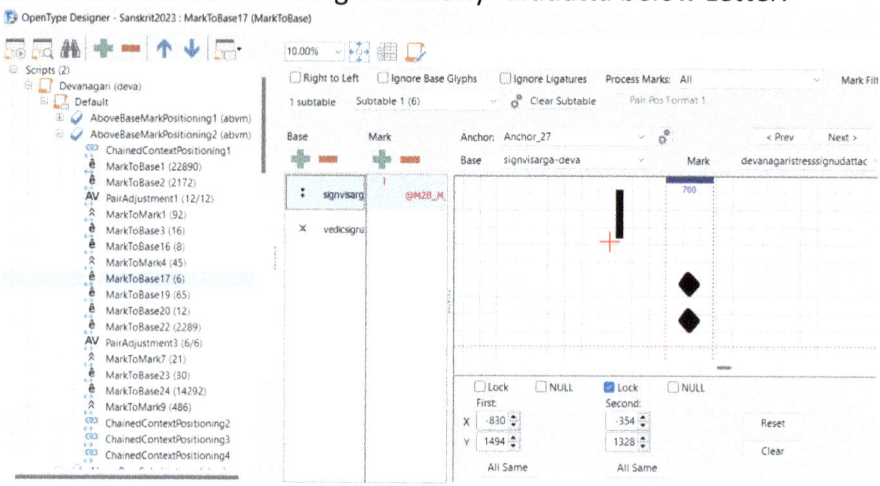

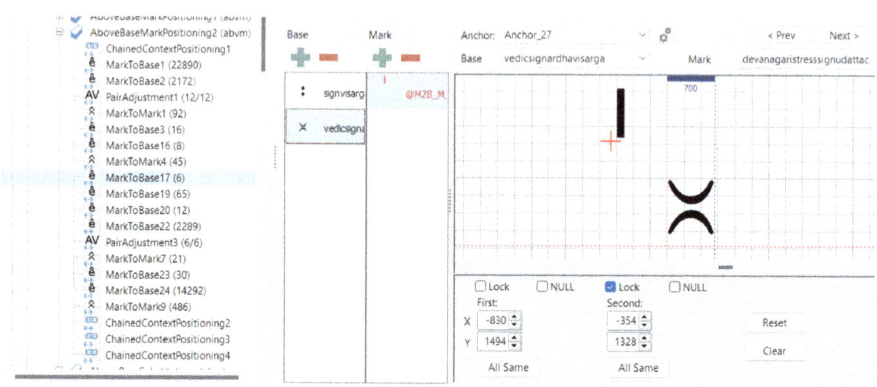

Note: The Indic Shaping properties for ardhavisarga are missing. To be implemented by the Shaping Engine or by Microsoft Word.

Note: As a workaround, we see that it gets typed correctly क॑ᳲ when we use Insert Symbol to type Svarita (and not directly from keyboard). Similarly क॒ᳲ

Feature = MarkToBase
MarkToBase – Adjusting the placement of glyphs from the Devanagari Extended block.

- Vowel and combining numeral ꣳ अ꣢

- Vowel and combining letter अ꣣ ओ꣱

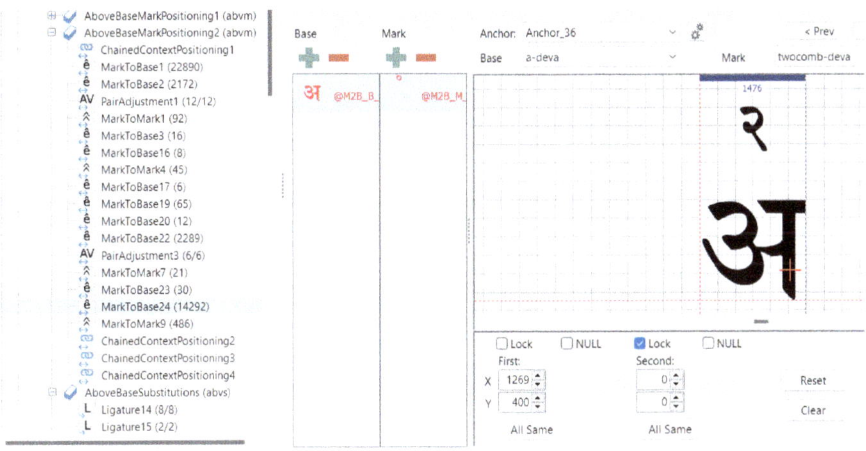

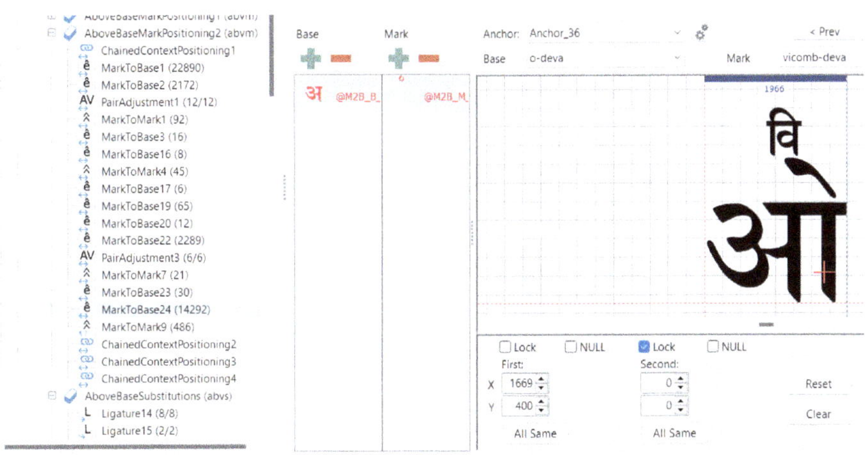

Feature = ChainedContextPositioning

ChainedContextPositioning – Adjusting the placement of three glyphs wrt each other.

- RephaHalant Letter Matra र्क ि → र्कि

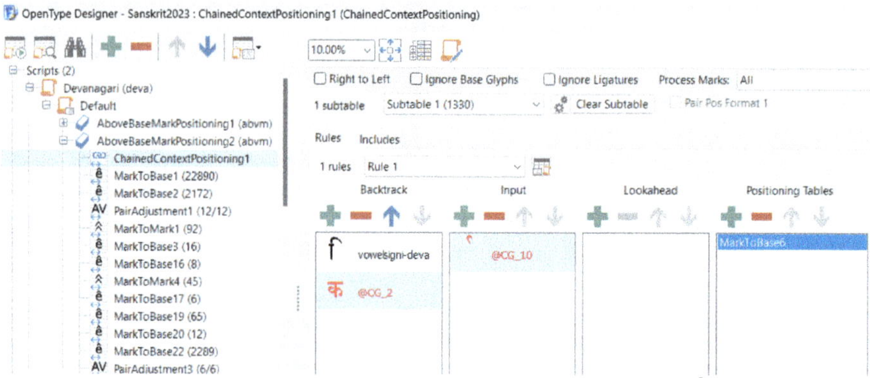

- RephaHalant Letter Matra Anusvara र्क ि ं → र्किं

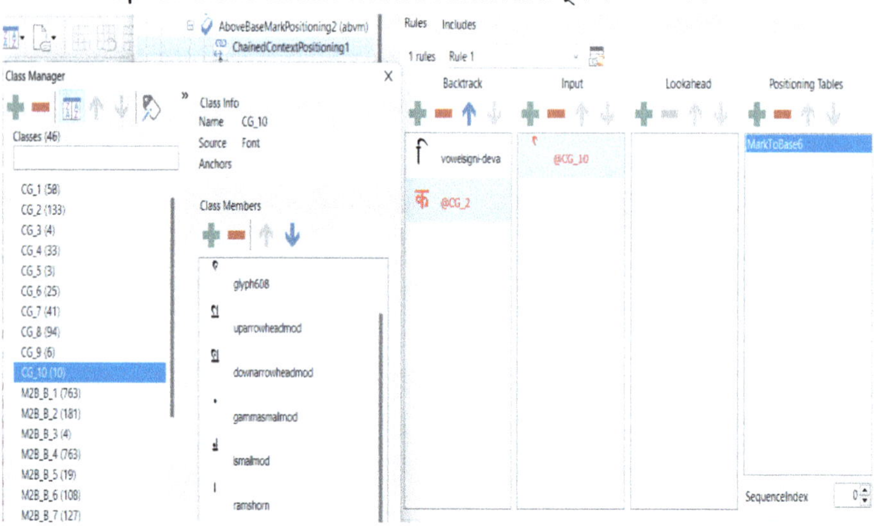

Class Manager for grouping glyphs with same Indic Shaping rules.

Note: Only three glyphs are in operation in this Feature, viz.

Backtrack = Matra glyph ि

Backtrack = Letter glyph क on which Matra shall attach

Input = The RephaHalant glyph

We use a Class Manager to group glyphs with similar operations.

Here CG_2 = array of glyphs (क ख ग घ etc.)

Here CG_10 = array of glyphs (etc.)

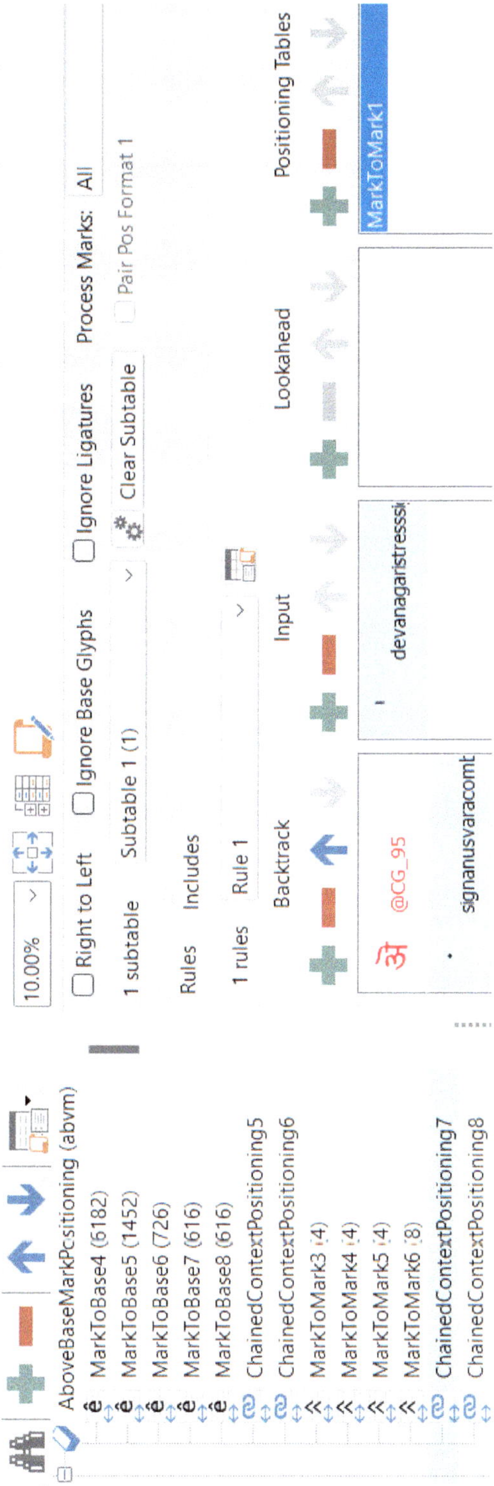
AboveBaseMarkPositioning (abvm)
MarkToBase4 (6182)
MarkToBase5 (1452)
MarkToBase6 (726)
MarkToBase7 (616)
MarkToBase8 (616)
ChainedContextPositioning5
ChainedContextPositioning6
MarkToMark3 (4)
MarkToMark4 (4)
MarkToMark5 (4)
MarkToMark6 (8)
ChainedContextPositioning7
ChainedContextPositioning8
10.00%
Right to Left
Ignore Base Glyphs
Ignore Ligatures
Process Marks:
All
1 subtable
Subtable 1 (1)
Clear Subtable
Pair Pos Format 1
Rules
Includes
1 rules
Rule 1
Backtrack
Input
Lookahead
Positioning Tables
अ
@CG_95
signanusvaracomb
devanagaristresssi
MarkToMark1

AboveBaseSubstitutions (abvs)

Feature = Ligature.

For replacing the combination of rephaHalant+matra glyphs with a new ligature. Otherwise it will be incorrectly positioned due to overlap.

E.g. rephaHalant+consonant+matra र्क ी → र्की

ी ी are new drawn Ligatures.

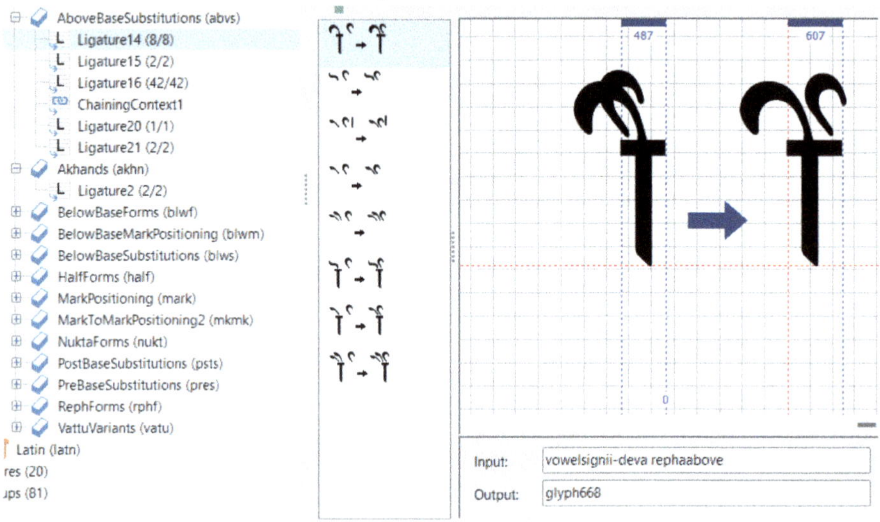

E.g. rephaHalant+vowel+candrabindu र्ई ँ → र्ईँ

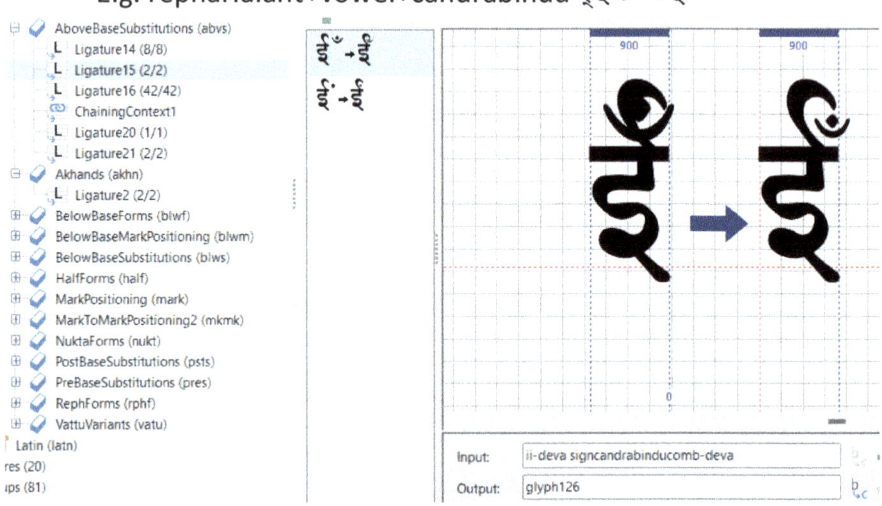

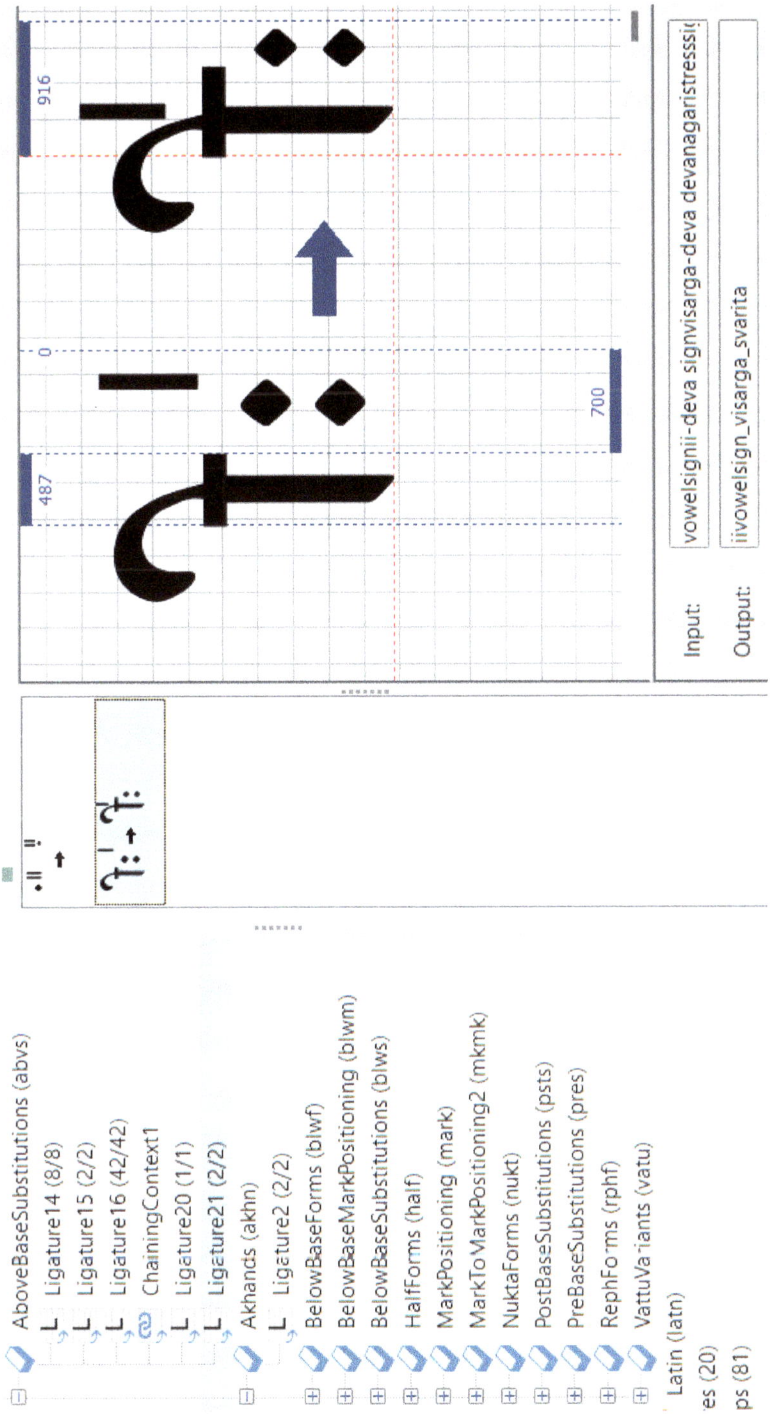

E.g. consonant+matra+visarga+svarita क ◌ी ◌ः ◌॑ → कीः॑

Akhands (akhn)

Feature = Ligature.
For replacing the combination of consonant+halant+consonant glyphs with a new ligature.
Used only for two ligatures called akhands, namely

क ◌् ष → क्ष where क्ष is a new Ligature.

ज ◌् ञ → ज्ञ where ज्ञ is a new Ligature.

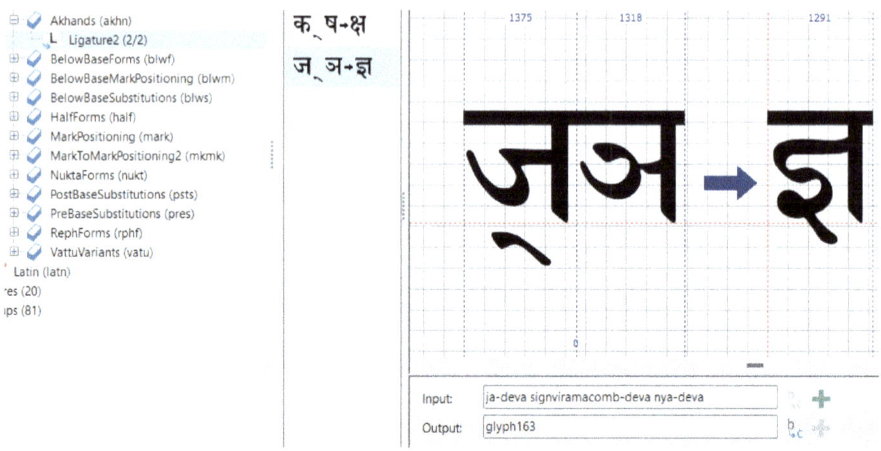

BelowBaseForms (blwf)

Feature = ChainingContext.

For replacing the combination of consonant+halant glyphs with a new ligature. E.g. क ् → क्र

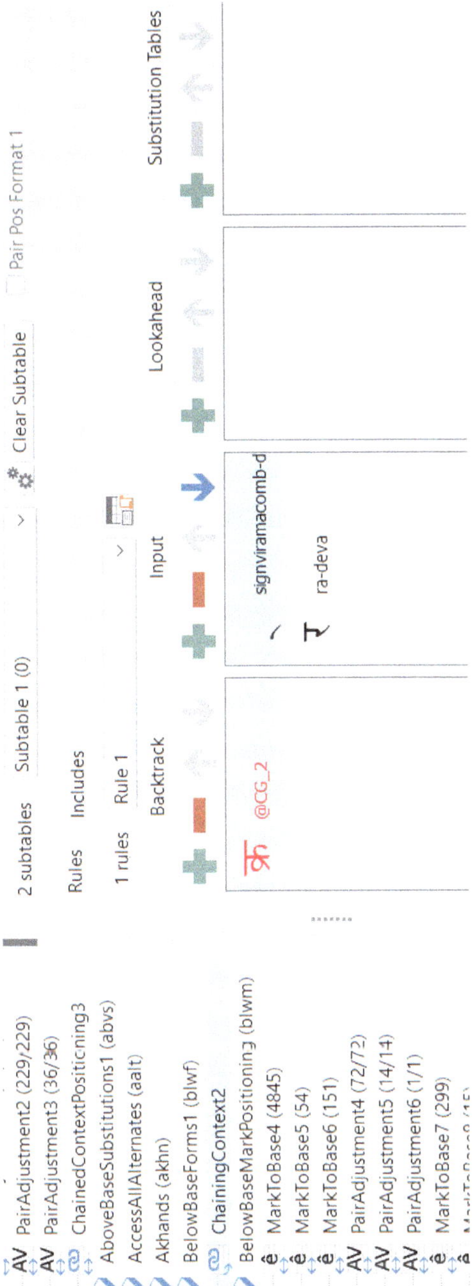

BelowBaseMarkPositioning (blwm)

Feature = MarkToBase

MarkToBase - Attaching anchor of such a mark glyph that must be attached below the base glyph. This works for **two independent glyphs**, and is used to adjust the relative position of both such that the final glyph is correct as per the Sanskrit literature.

Firstly, we need to specify the dotted circle glyph for all below base marks, that should be inserted in case a required base glyph is absent.

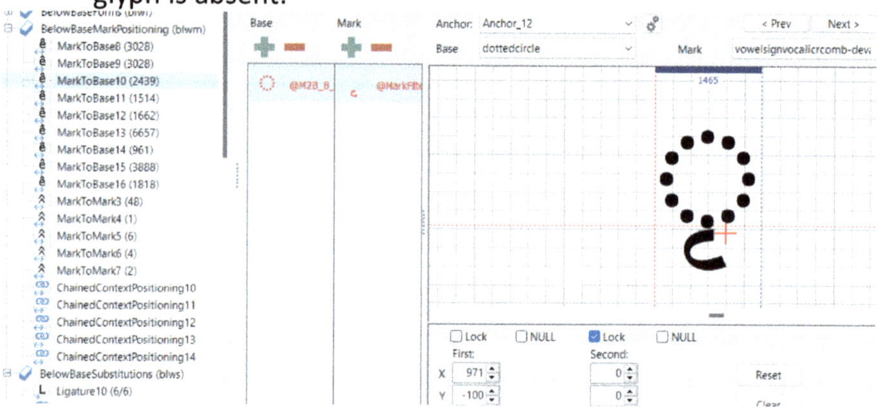

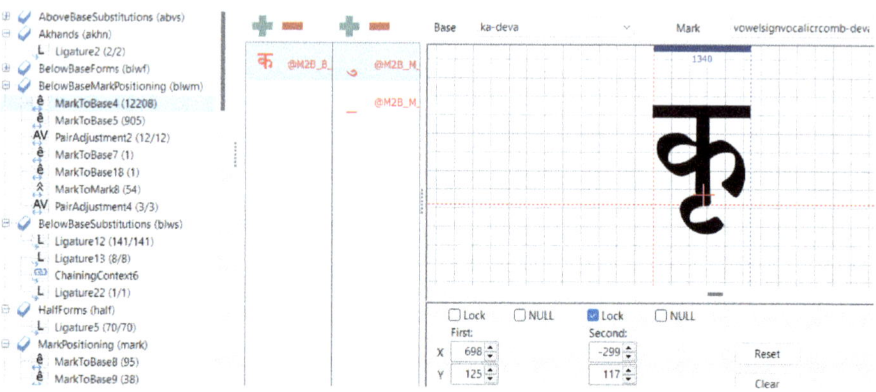

Below mark glyphs array ◌ु ◌ू ◌ृ ◌ॄ ◌॒ ◌ॢ ◌ॣ Devanagari Block.

Below mark glyphs array ◌᳕ ◌᳖ ◌᳗ ◌᳘ ◌᳙ ◌᳜ ◌᳝ ◌᳞ ◌᳟ VedicExtensions.

Feature = MarkToMark

MarkToMark - Adjusting the precise position of two mark glyphs wrt each other that are placed below a base glyph.

e.g. Letter+uMatra+anudattaAccent

All three glyphs are from Devanagari block. क ◌ु ◌॒ → कु॒

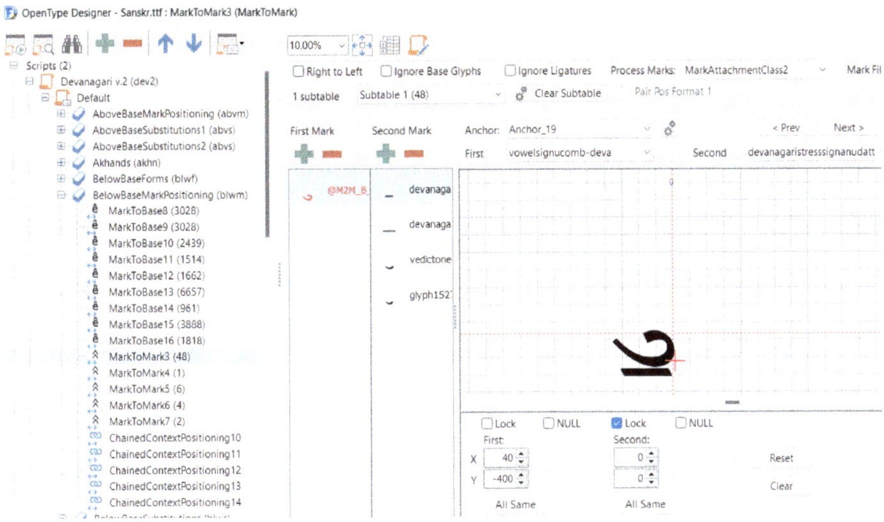

Glyphs are from Devanagari and VedicExtensions. क ◌ू ◌᳘ → कू᳘

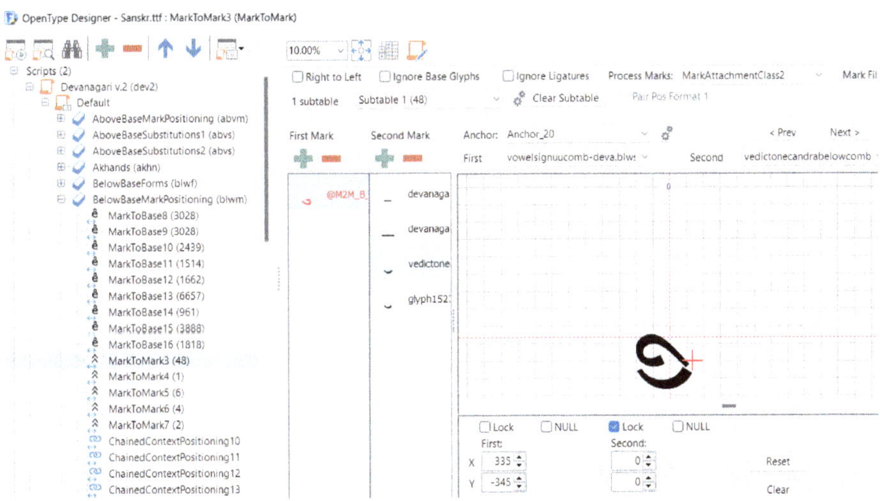

Feature = PairAdjustment

PairAdjustment - Adjusting the precise position of two mark glyphs wrt each other that are placed below a base glyph.

e.g. Letter+uMatra+anudattaAccent

All three glyphs are from Devanagari block. क ◌ु ◌॒ → कु॒

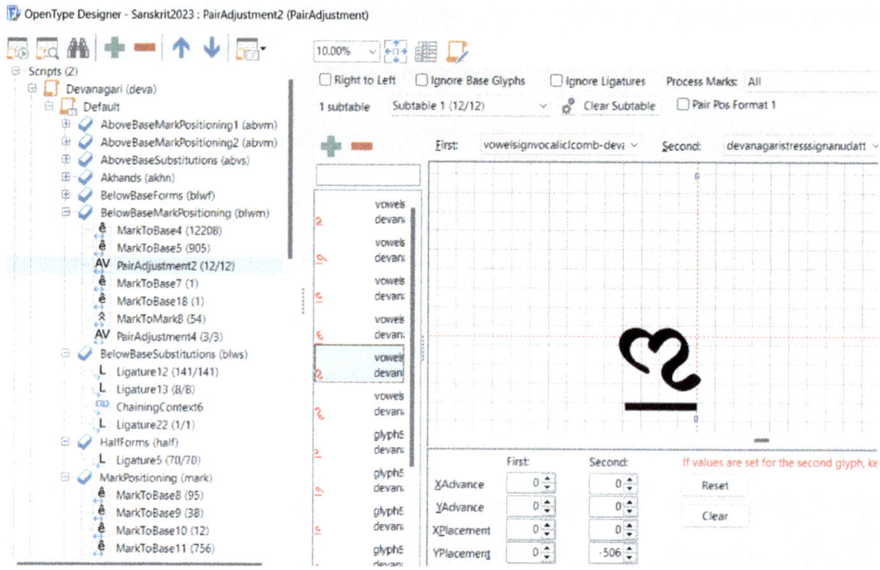

Question: Should we use MarkToMark here?

What actually works? MarkToMark or PairAdjustment?

The fonts SanskritText and AdobeDevanagari do not use PairAdjustment feature here. MarkToMark is used.

Feature = MarkToBase

MarkToBase - Attaching anchor of such a mark glyph that must be attached below the base glyph. This works for **two independent glyphs**, and is used to adjust the relative position of both such that the final glyph is correct as per the Sanskrit literature.

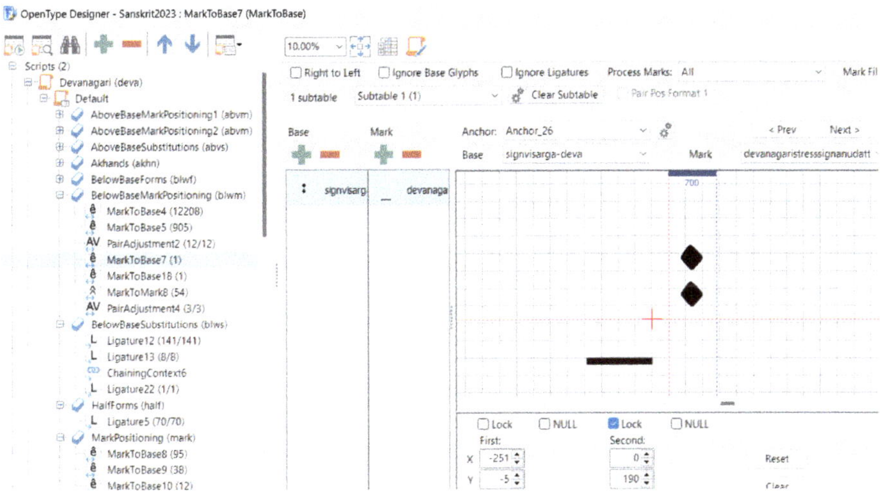

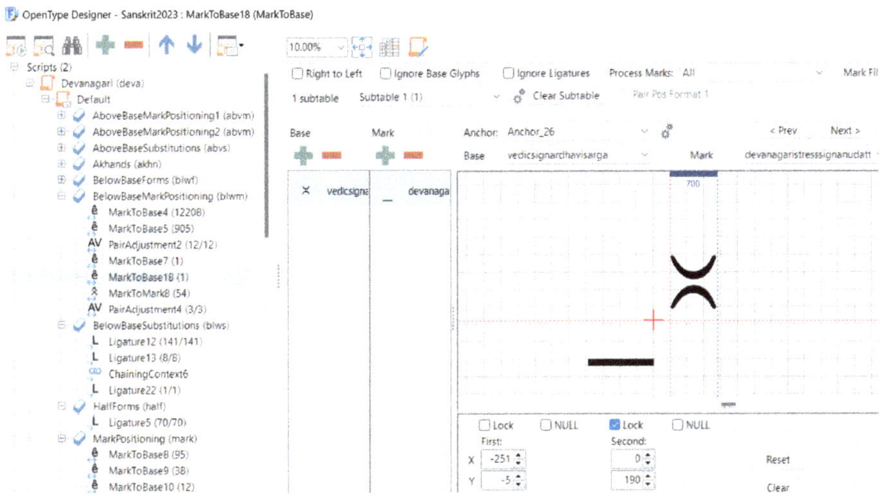

Proposal: Ardhavisarga needs to be implemented for it to work.

Question: Should we use MarkToMark here?

BelowBaseSubstitutions (blws)

Feature = Ligature

Ligature - Attaching anchor of such a mark glyph that must be attached below the base glyph. This works for **two independent glyphs**, and is used to adjust the relative position of both such that the final glyph is correct as per the Sanskrit literature.

Ligature-replacing overlapping glyphs with new drawn glyph that do not overlap.

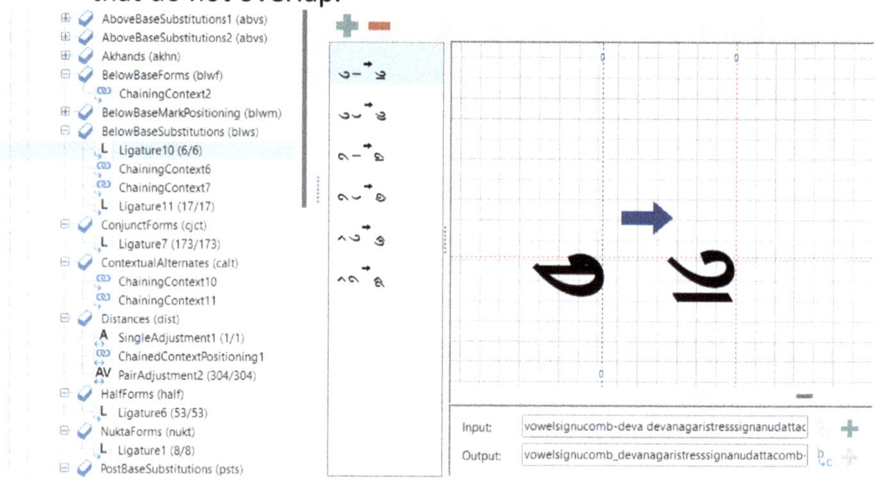

Question: SanskritText font uses both blwm and blws in this present case? Why? BelowBaseMarkPositioning with feature MarkToMark / BelowBaseSubstitutions with feature Ligature.

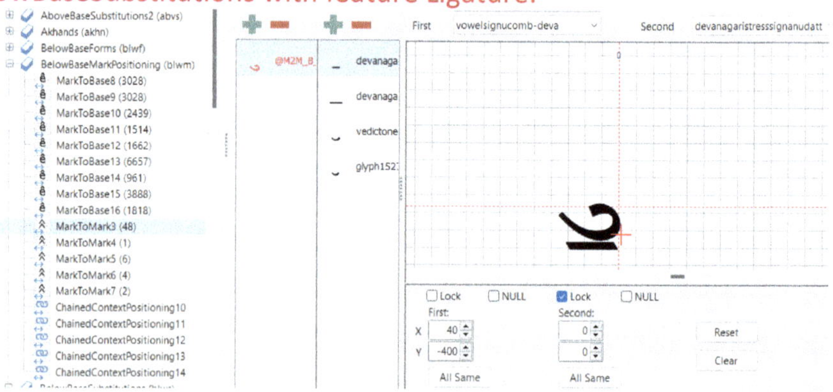

Note: AdobeDevanagari font uses only blwm in this present case.

ट ◌ु ◌॒ → टु॒ (टु॒ Sanskrit2023 needs rectification)

BelowBaseMarkPositioning with feature MarkToMark.

But for this case it uses the BelowBaseSubstitutions with feature Ligature.

ट ◌् र ◌ु → ट्रु

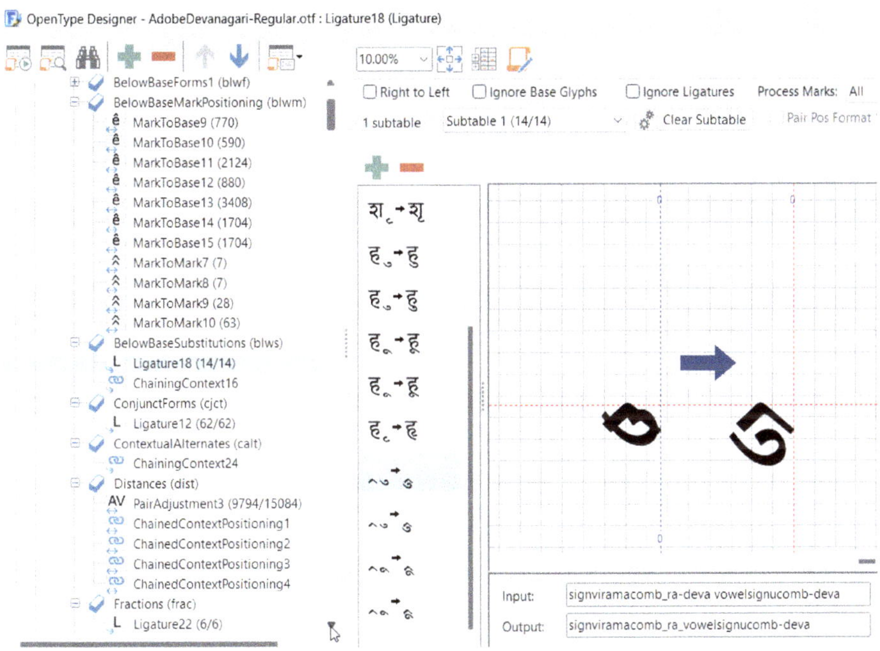

टु॒ टु॒ टु॒ Annapurna SIL टु॒

Feature = Ligature.

For replacing the combination of repha+uMatra glyphs with a new ligature.

E.g. र ◌ु → रु

र ◌ू → रू

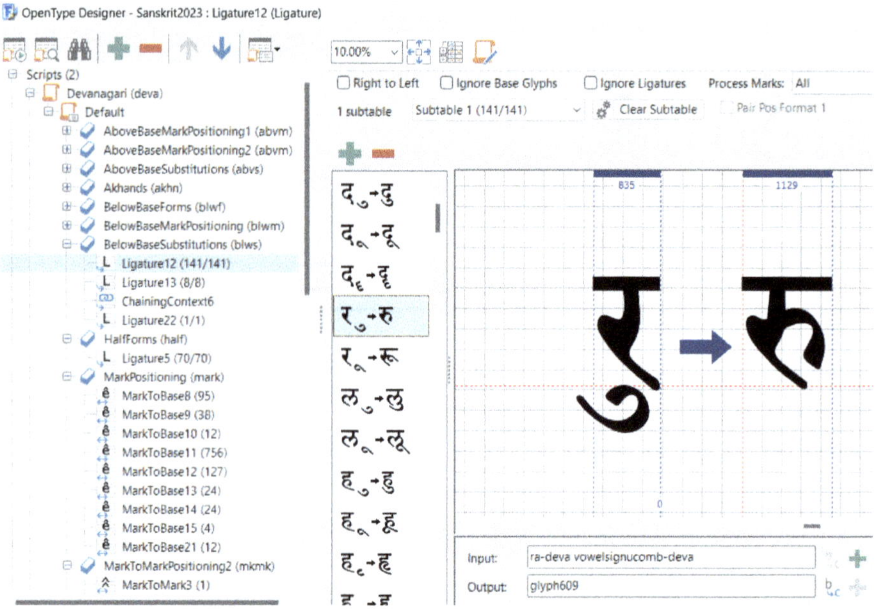

Also other glyphs where neatness or specific ligature is desired.

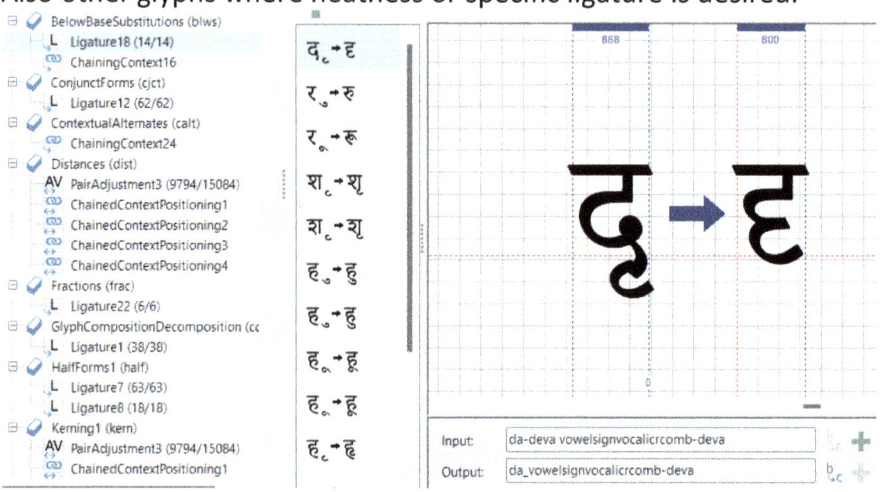

ConjunctForms (cjct)

Feature = Ligature.
For replacing the combination of consonant+halant+consonant glyphs with a new conjunct ligature found in literature.

E.g. क ् क → क्क where क्क is a new Ligature.

ङ ् क → ङ्क where ङ्क is a new Ligature.

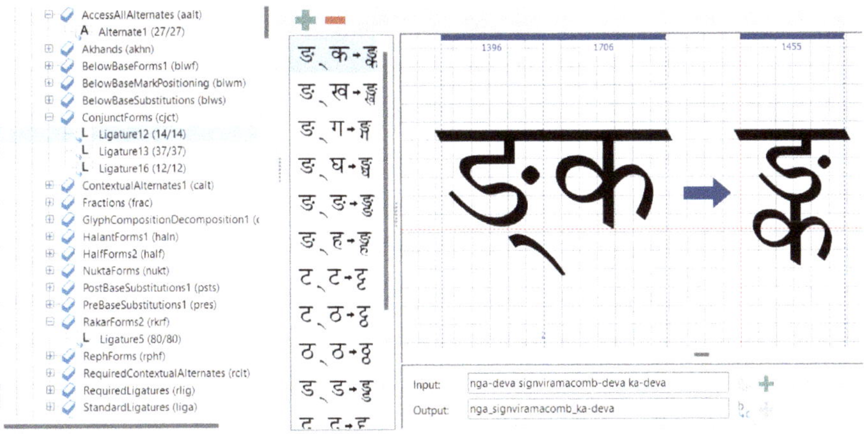

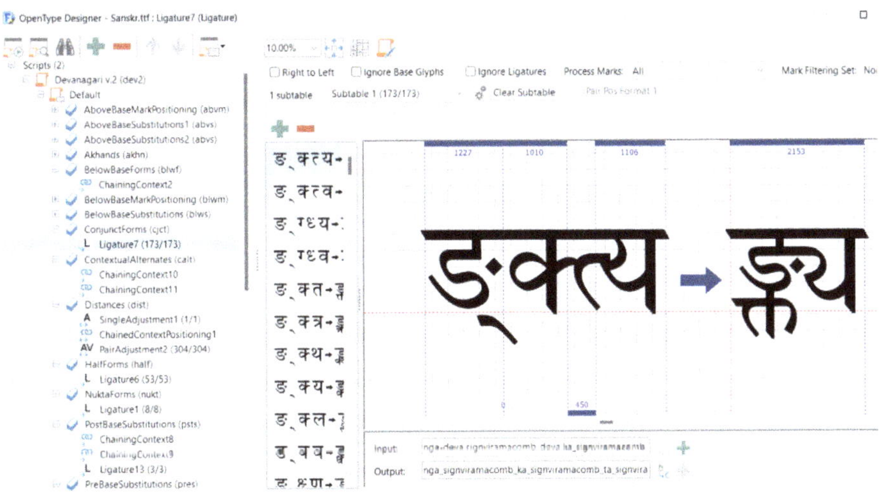

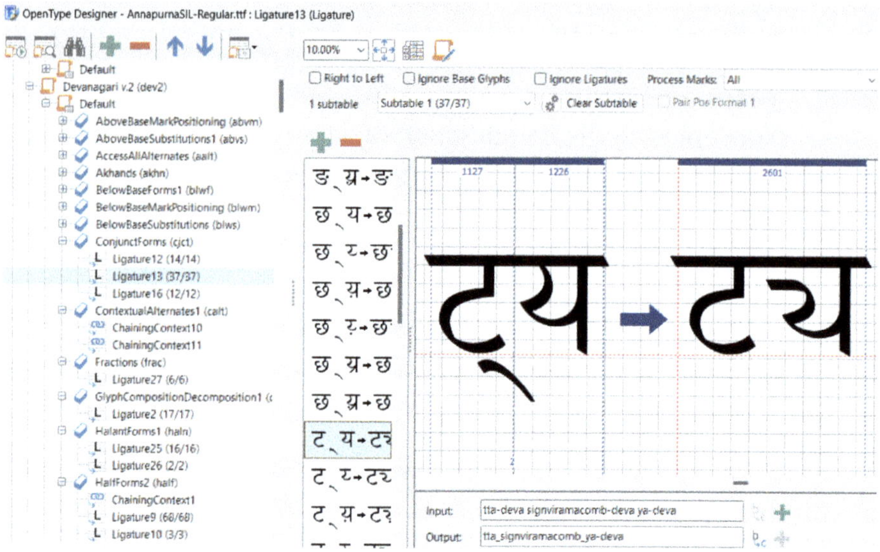

Feature = ChainingContext.

For replacing the combination of glyphs with a new ligature.

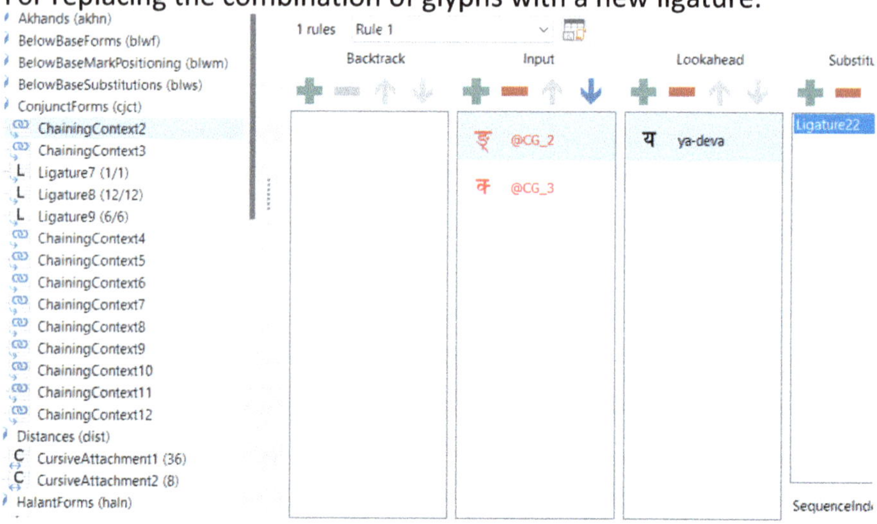

HalantForms (haln)

Feature = Ligature.

For replacing the combination of consonant+halant glyphs with a new ligature where halant is well positioned.

E.g. ढ ◌् → ढ् where ढ् is a new Ligature.

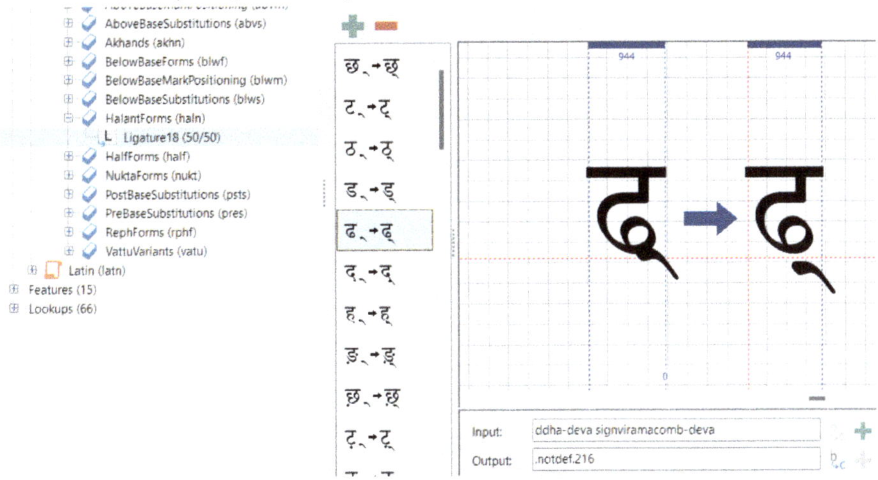

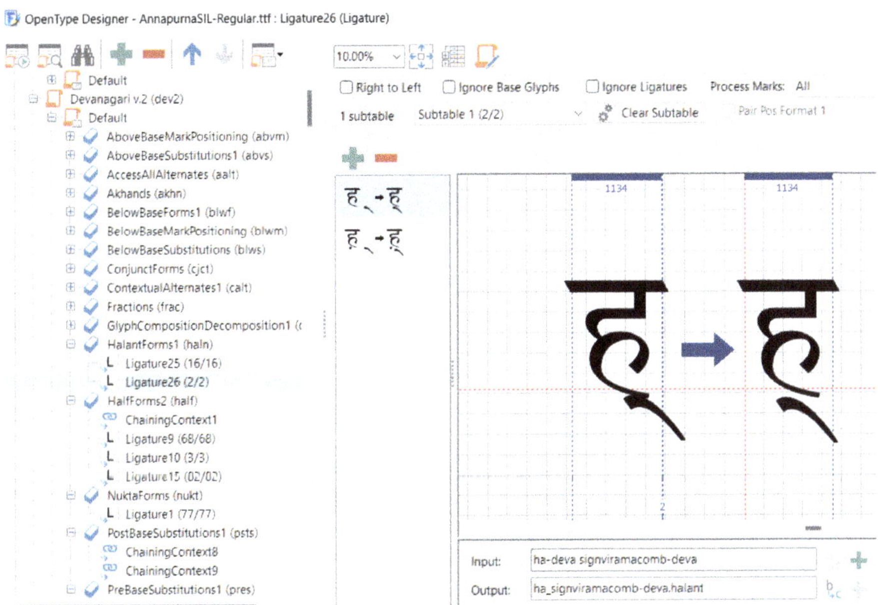

HalfForms (half)

Feature = Ligature.

For replacing the combination of consonant+halant glyphs with a new half-consonant ligature.

E.g. क ् → क्‍ where क्‍ is a new Ligature.

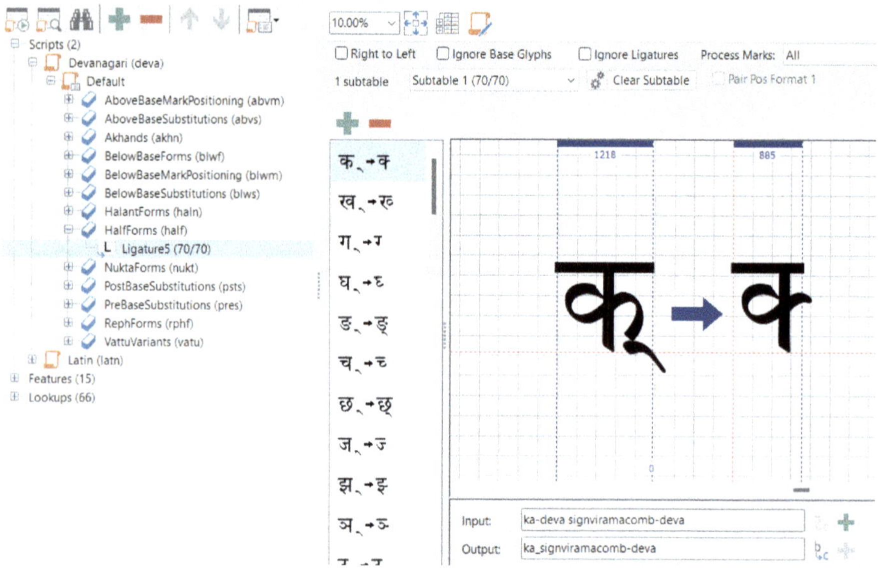

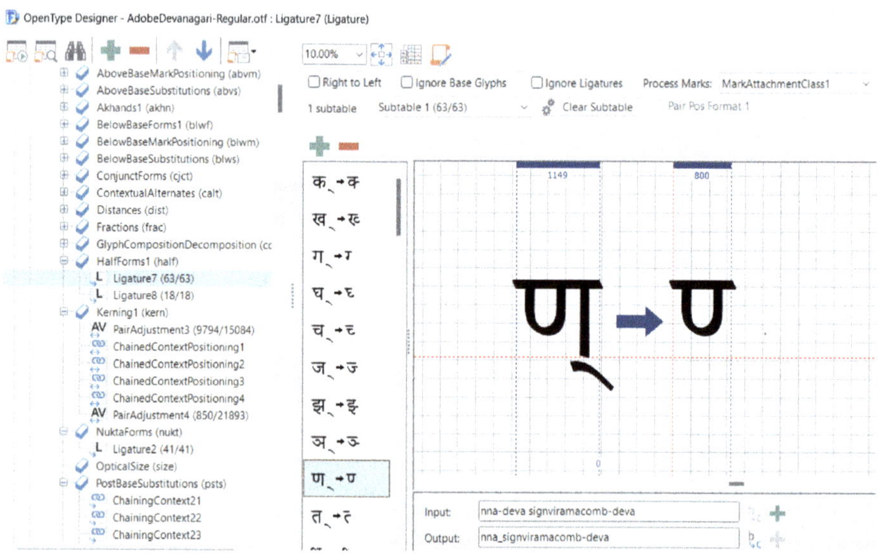

MarkPositioning (mark)

MarkToMarkPositioning (mkmk)

https://learn.microsoft.com/en-us/typography/opentype/spec/features_ko

NuktaForms (nukt)

Feature = Ligature.
For replacing the combination of consonant+nukta glyphs with a new ligature.

E.g. ज◌़ → ज़ where ज़ is a new Ligature with nukta correctly placed. Used only for Consonants कखगजडढफयरळ

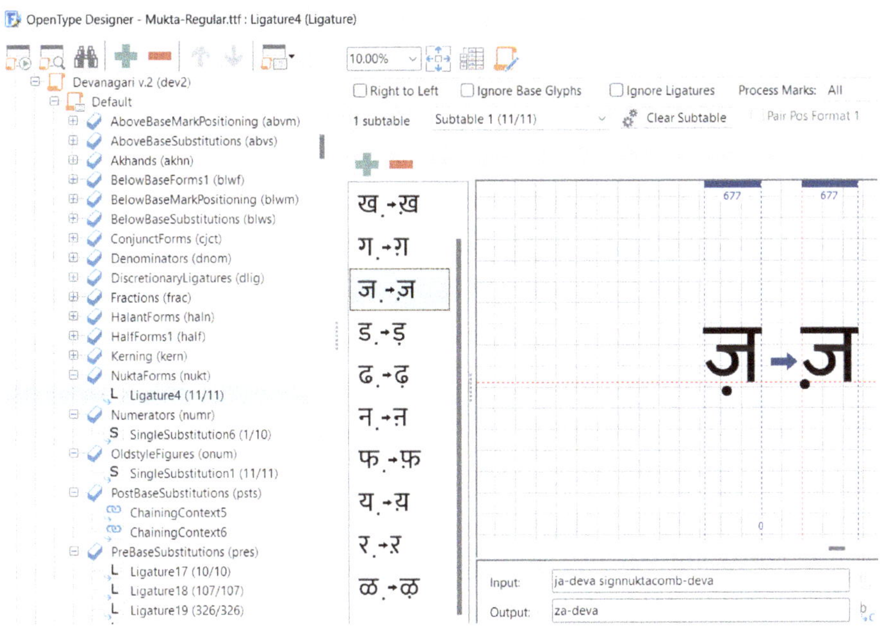

PostBaseSubstitutions (psts)

Feature = Ligature.

For replacing the combination of consonant+halant glyphs with a new ligature.

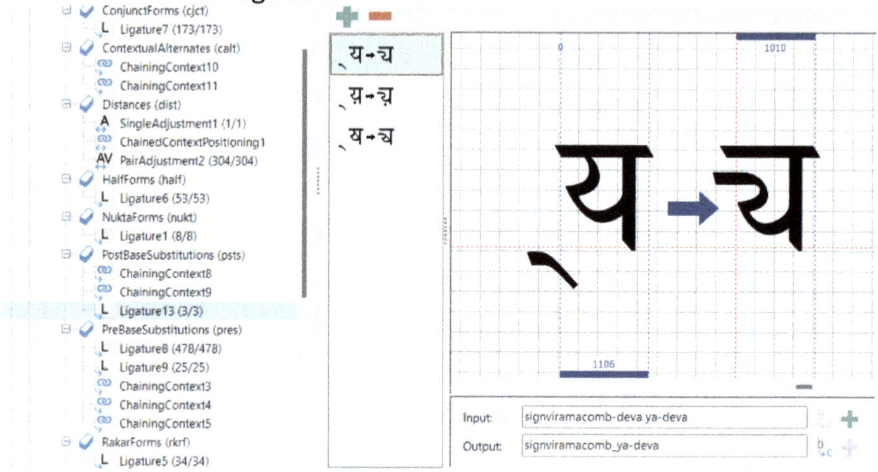

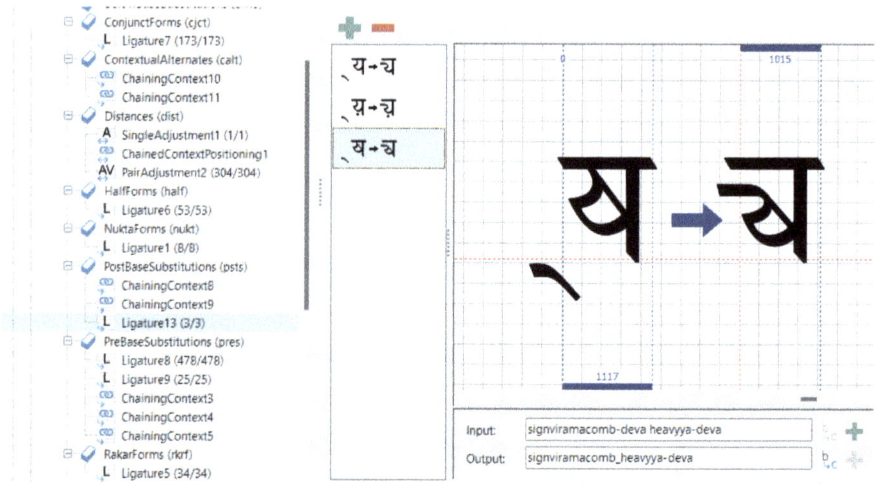

This feature replaces post-base-consonant glyphs with special ligatures. E.g. stylistic variants of right-side matra.

फ ◌ी → फी → फी

Feature = ChainingContext.
For replacing the combination of consonant+iMatra glyphs with a new ligature having correctly shaped iMatra.

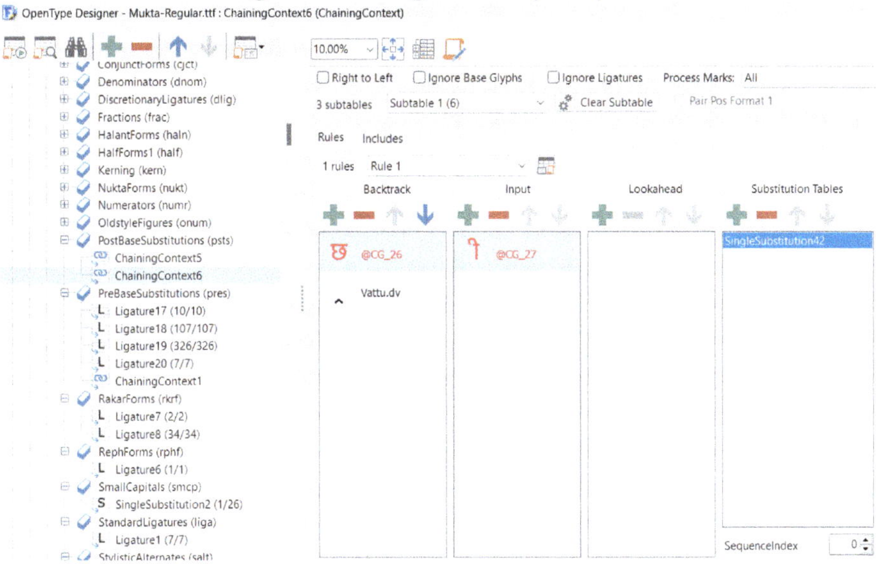

PreBaseSubstitutions (pres)

Feature = Ligature.
For replacing the combination of consonant+halant+consonant glyphs with a new ligature.

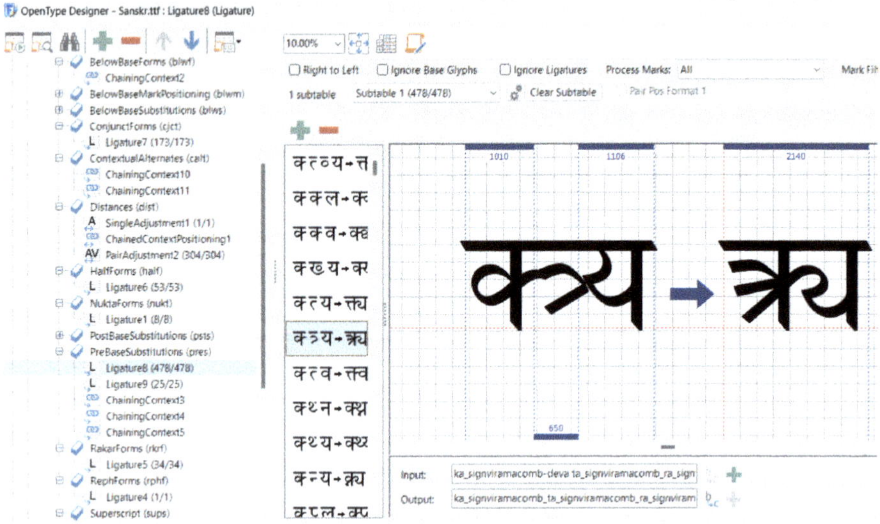

This feature replaces pre-base-consonant glyphs with special ligatures. E.g. stylistic variants of left-side matra.

ख ि → खि → खि

Feature = ChainingContext.
For replacing the combination of consonant+iMatra glyphs with a new ligature having correctly shaped iMatra.

RakarForms (rkrf)

Feature = Ligature.

Ligature-replacing consonant+halant+repha combination glyphs with new drawn Ligature conjunct having back slash for repha. E.g. क ् र → क्र where क्र is a new Ligature. (Not used in ट ् र → ट्र where the repha becomes a caret i.e. circumflex, below some Consonants. For that the Feature = VattuVariants is used).

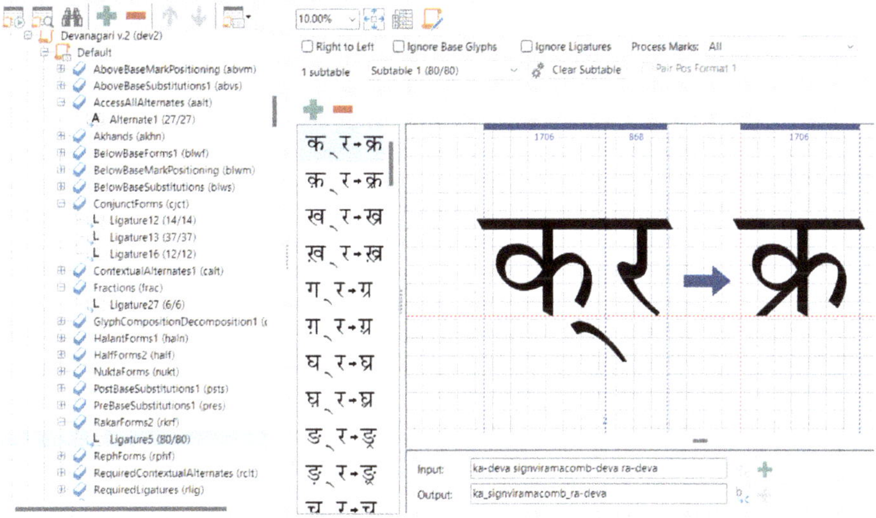

RephForms (rphf)

Feature = Ligature.
Ligature for replacing repha+halant glyphs with top curl glyph. Only this one Ligature र◌्→

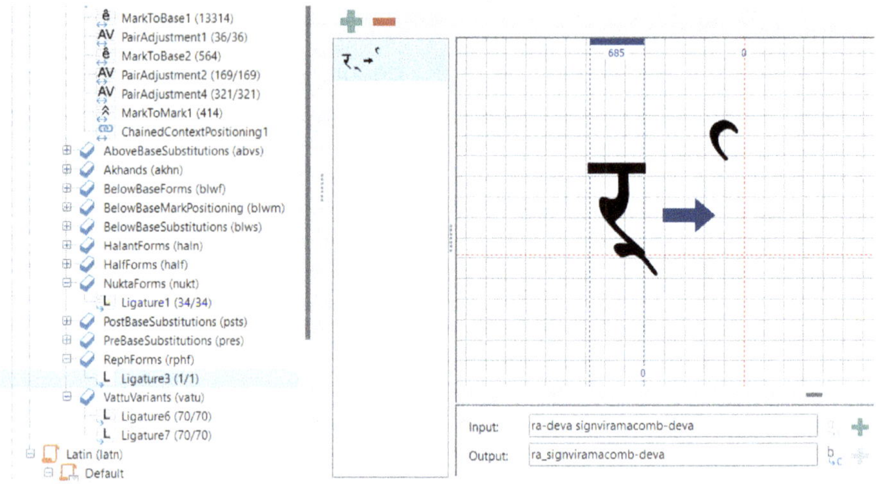

VattuVariants (vatu)

Ligature-replacing consonant+halant+repha combination glyphs with new drawn Ligature conjunct having caret below for repha. E.g. ट◌्र→ट्र where ट्र is a new Ligature.

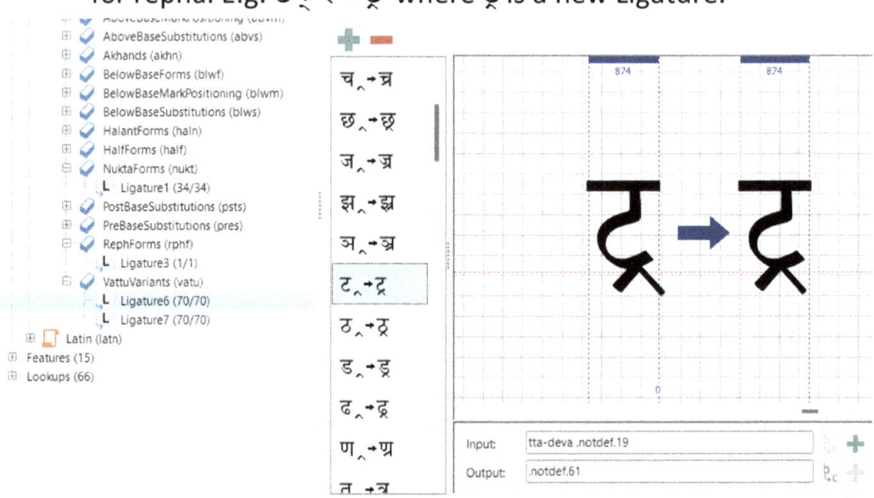

StylisticAlternates (salt)

Feature = SingleSubstitution.

Replacing a glyph with another glyph, for presentation.

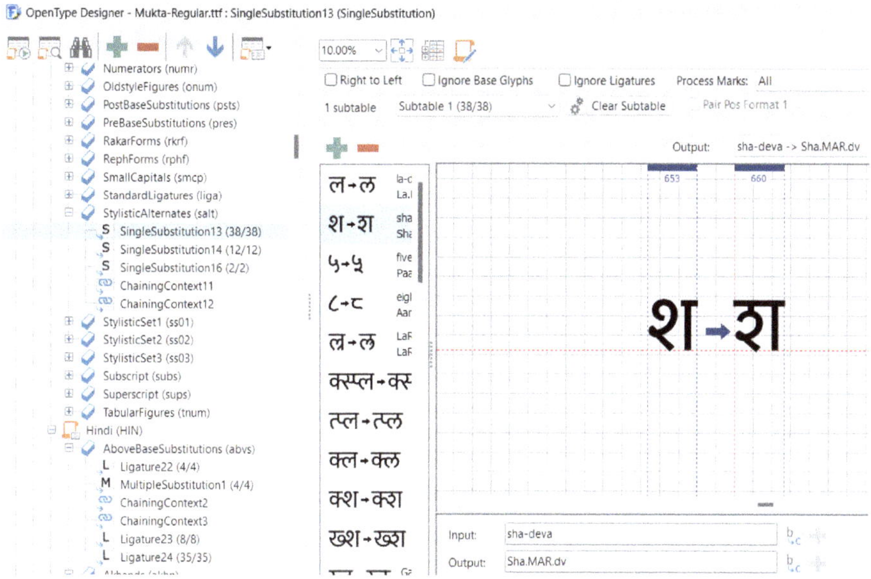

StylisticSet (ss)

Feature = SingleSubstitution.

Replacing a glyph with another glyph, for archaic use presentation.

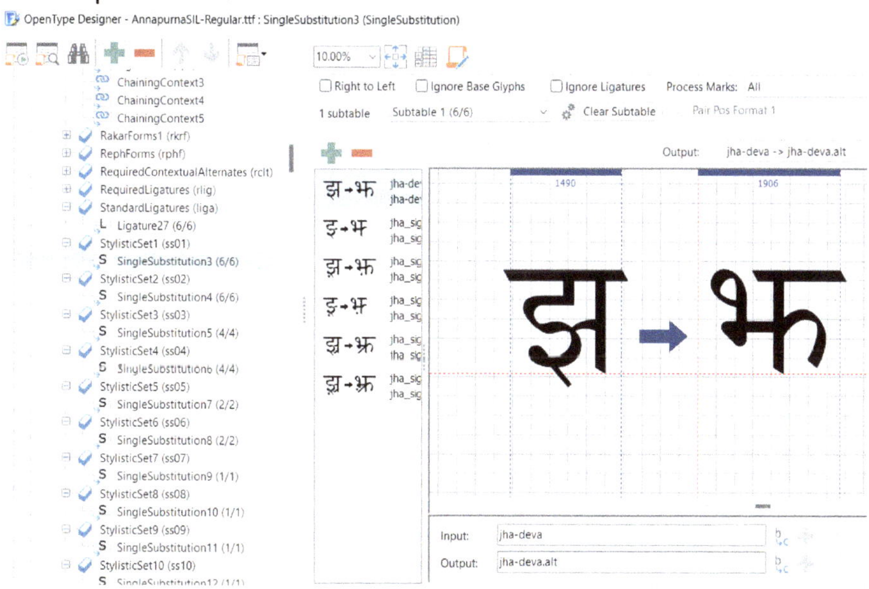

Kerning (kern)

Feature = PairAdjustment.

Adjusting gap between glyphs.

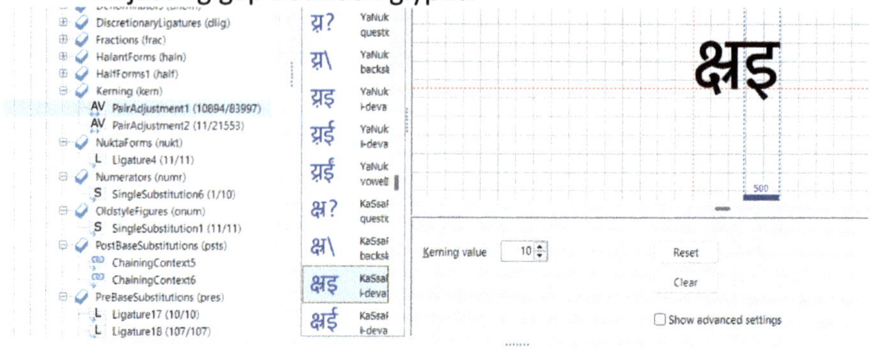

Distances (dist)

Feature = CursiveAttachment.

Adjusting gap between glyphs.

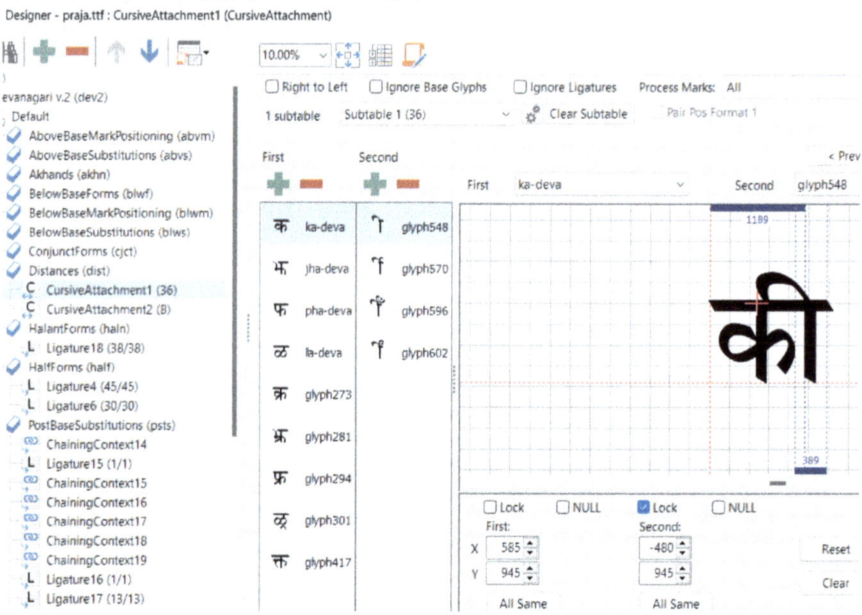

Devanagari Character Glyph Class Scheme

An important part of Devanagari Font creation is knowing the class of each glyph and character from Unicode Block. Then we can attach and position them correctly.

A proposed character class scheme for correct implementation of Sanskrit Typesetting is outlined here, so that

- Unicode Developers
- Script Developers
- Font Developers
- Open Type Design Shaping Engine Developers

can help users in writing "correct and beautiful Sanskrit" texts and books and documents as per the extant Ancient Sanskrit Literature, in the modern world.

The following is a proposed class scheme for the principal Devanagari Unicode Blocks used by any Sanskrit font.

NS = **Not in Sanskrit** usage/Dravidian etc.

IU = Indirect Use.

V = Vowel.

C = **Consonant** with inherent vowel.

M = **Matra** of Vowel Sign. Only one Matra out of the set can be attached to a Consonant or Conjunct.

N = **Nasalization** or Visarga Sign. Can attach to Vowel or Consonant or Conjunct, with or without Matra. Only one of these can attach simultaneously.

A = **Accent** or Stress Sign. Only one Accent out of the set can be attached to a Vowel or Consonant, with or without Matra.

S = **Sandhi** Symbol.

P = **Punctuation** Symbol.

OM = Sacred Symbol.

E = **Extended Nukta** Sign. Can attach to a Consonant with or without Matra.

H = Vowel Suppress **Halant** Sign. Can attach only to a Consonant.

O = **Numeral**. Ordinal.

IU = Insignificant Use Consonant.

In a Open type design software,
the Symbols are independent glyphs, while
the Signs are dependent glyphs.

Hence when we insert a Symbol in MS Word, it is directly typed. However when we insert a Sign in MS Word it is seen with a geometric shape dotted circle, to signify that some other glyph should precede it first, and it will attach to that glyph.

Make new glyphs in Sanskrit 2023 for signs with dotted circle.

Devanagari Block = Unicode U+0900 to 097F

128 characters with glyphs

0900	0901	0902	0903	0904	0905	0906	0907
◌ऀ	◌ँ	◌ं	◌ः	ऄ	अ	आ	इ
N	N	N	N	NS	V	V	V

0908	0909	090A	090B	090C	090D	090E	090F
ई	उ	ऊ	ऋ	ऌ	ऍ	ऎ	ए
V	V	V	V	V	NS	NS	V

0910	0911	0912	0913	0914	0915	0916	0917
ऐ	ऑ	ऒ	ओ	औ	क	ख	ग
V	NS	NS	V	V	C	C	C

0918	0919	091A	091B	091C	091D	091E	091F
घ	ङ	च	छ	ज	झ	ञ	ट
C	C	C	C	C	C	C	C

0920	0921	0922	0923	0924	0925	0926	0927
ठ	ड	ढ	ण	त	थ	द	ध
C	C	C	C	C	C	C	C

0928	0929	092A	092B	092C	092D	092E	092F
न	ऩ	प	फ	ब	भ	म	य
C	C	C	C	C	C	C	C

0930	0931	0932	0933	0934	0935	0936	0937
र	ऱ	ल	ळ	ऴ	व	श	ष
C	NS	C	C	NS	C	C	C

0938	0939	093A	093B	093C	093D	093E	093F
स	ह	◌ऺ	◌ऻ	◌़	ऽ	◌ा	◌ि
C	C	NS	NS	E	S	M	M

0940	0941	0942	0943	0944	0945	0946	0947
◌ी	◌ु	◌ू	◌ृ	◌ॄ	◌ॅ	◌ॆ	◌े
M	M	M	M	M	NS	NS	M

0948	0949	094A	094B	094C	094D	094E	094F
◌ै	◌ॉ	◌ॊ	◌ो	◌ौ	◌्	◌ॎ	◌ॏ
M	NS	NS	M	M	H	NS	NS

0950	0951	0952	0953	0954	0955	0956	0957
ॐ	॑	॒	॓	॔	◌ॕ	◌ॖ	◌ॗ
OM	A	A	NS	NS	NS	NS	NS

0958	0959	095A	095B	095C	095D	095E	095F
क़	ख़	ग़	ज़	ड़	ढ़	फ़	य़
IU	IU	IU	IU	IU	IU	IU	IU

0960	0961	0962	0963	0964	0965	0966	0967
ॠ	ॡ	◌ॢ	◌ॣ	।	॥	०	१
V	V	M	M	P	P	O	O

0968	0969	096A	096B	096C	096D	096E	096F
२	३	४	५	६	७	८	९
O	O	O	O	O	O	O	O

0970	0971	0972	0973	0974	0975	0976	0977
॰	ॱ	ॲ	ॳ	ॴ	ॵ	ॶ	ॷ
P	P	NS	NS	NS	NS	NS	NS

0978	0979	097A	097B	097C	097D	097E	097F
ॸ	ॹ	ॺ	ॻ	ॼ	ॽ	ॾ	ॿ
NS	NS	C	NS	NS	NS	NS	NS

Vedic Extensions Block = Unicode 1CD0 to 1CFF

48 characters with 43 glyphs and last 5 Unallocated.

Legend

AO = **Accent On Numeral** Sign. Usually attaches to Numerals.

VA = **Visarga Accent** Sign. Can attach only to Visarga.

GA = **Gomukha Anusvara** Symbol. Long Anusvara Symbol. Usually the Anusvara Sign is additionally attached to a Gomukha. Refer Combining Diacritical Marks Supplement Block.

GT = **Gomukha Tiryak** Sign. Can attach only to a Gomukha.

SA = Special Anusvara Symbol.

P = Punctuation Symbol.

A = **Accent** Sign. Stress Sign.

NS = **Not in Sanskrit** Language. Used in Dravidian, Bhojpuri etc.

1CD0	1CD1	1CD2	1CD3	1CD4	1CD5	1CD6	1CD7
᳐	᳑	᳒	᳓	᳔	᳕	᳖	᳗
AO	AO	AO	P	A	A	A	A

1CD8	1CD9	1CDA	1CDB	1CDC	1CDD	1CDE	1CDF
᳘	᳙	᳚	᳛	᳜	᳝	᳞	᳟
A	A	A	A	A	A	A	A

1CE0	1CE1	1CE2	1CE3	1CE4	1CE5	1CE6	1CE7
᳠	᳡	᳢	᳣	᳤	᳥	᳦	᳧
NS	P	VA	VA	VA	VA	VA	VA

1CE8	1CE9	1CEA	1CEB	1CEC	1CED	1CEE	1CEF
᳨	ᳩ	ᳪ	ᳫ	ᳬ	᳭	ᳮ	ᳯ
VA	GA	GA	GA	GA	GT	SA	SA

1CF0	1CF1	1CF2	1CF3	1CF4	1CF5	1CF6	1CF7
ᳰ	ᳱ	ᳲ	ᳳ	᳴	ᳵ	ᳶ	᳷
SA	SA	N	N	A	NS	NS	P

1CF8	1CF9	1CFA	1CFB	1CFC	1CFD	1CFE	1CFF
᳸	᳹	ᳺ					
A	A	GA					

Devanagari Extended Block = Unicode A8E0 to A8FF

32 characters with glyphs.

Legend

AV = Samaveda Accent Sign. AV signs are Accents attached above. To Vowels; and Consonants with Inherent vowel, with or without Matra. These are non-spacing signs.

IN = Independent Nasal Anusvara Symbol.

AH = Headstroke Accent Sign.

SS = Sacred Siddham Symbol.

P = Punctuation Symbol.

NS = **Not in Sanskrit** Language. Used in Dravidian, Bhojpuri etc.

A8E0	A8E1	A8E2	A8E3	A8E4	A8E5	A8E6	A8E7
◌꣠	◌꣡	◌꣢	◌꣣	◌꣤	◌꣥	◌꣦	◌꣧
AV	AV	AV	AV	AV	AV	AV	AV

A8E8	A8E9	A8EA	A8EB	A8EC	A8ED	A8EE	A8EF
◌꣨	◌꣩	◌꣪	◌꣫	◌꣬	◌꣭	◌꣮	◌꣯
AV	AV	AV	AV	AV	AV	AV	AV

AV signs are Accents attached above to

- Vowels and
- Consonants with Inherent vowel, with or without Matra.

A8F0	A8F1	A8F2	A8F3	A8F4	A8F5	A8F6	A8F7
◌꣰	◌꣱	ꣲ	ꣳ	ꣴ	ꣵ	ꣶ	ꣷ
AV	AV	IN	IN	IN	IN	IN	IN

A8F8	A8F9	A8FA	A8FB	A8FC	A8FD	A8FE	A8FF
꣸	꣹	꣺	ꣻ	꣼	ꣽ	ꣾ	ꣿ
P	P	P	AH	SS	NS	NS	NS

अ आ इ ई उ ऊ ऋ ॠ ऌ ॡ ए ऐ ओ औ अं अः ।

अ॒ अ॑ अँ अं अः Devanagari

अ᳕ अ᳖ अ᳗ अ᳘ अ᳙ अ᳚ अ᳛ अ᳜ अ᳝ अ᳞ अ᳟ अᳵ अᳶ अ᳴ अ᳸ अ᳹

Vedic Extensions

अ꣡ अ꣢ अ꣣ अ꣤ अ꣥ अ꣦ अ꣧ अ꣨ अ꣩ अ꣠ अ꣪ अ꣫ अ꣬ अ꣭ अ꣮ अ꣯ अ꣰ अ꣱ अ꣺

अꣳ Devanagari Extended

Font Programming - Correct placement of Accent, Matra, Bindu, Nukta using Anchors

Software/ platform	Apple mac	Microsoft Word	LibreOffice	Google Android
Shaping engine	Coretext ???	Uniscribe/Dwrite	harfbuzz	harfbuzz

Any Unicode character is a glyph (symbol). To see its exact place in the Unicode character set, in hexadecimal.	The character code, ALT+X For example, to insert the euro currency symbol €, press **20AC**, and then hold down the ALT key and press X.

Note

- pres, psts, mkmk, mark are standard OpenTypeDesign Features whereas
- blws, abvs, psts, abvm, blwm are specific to Indic Language design support only

Implementation in font design using high-logic font editor.

- Position anchors in the Glyphs window and not in OpenType designer. Fine tune the anchors if needed in the designer.
- Search for anchors using find in code editor in designer.
- Associated Anchors will have an arrow mark. Unassociated anchors will have no mark, as seen in Anchors window.
- Each base glyph has an anchor point that is defined with the

  left X and Y value and is indicated by the anchor icon: Modifying these values will change the location of the mark glyph.
- Each mark glyph also has an anchor point that is defined with the right X and Y value. Modifying these values will change the location where the mark glyph will be drawn in relation to the base glyph anchor.

In short:

- Modify left X,Y: Change position of all marks in relation to the base glyph
- Modify right X,Y: Change position of mark in relation to all base glyphs

Note:

- For vowels with inbuilt top matra ii ई, ai ऐ, o ओ, au औ we may use new glyph ligature substitution if needed.
- For r+u र ु, r+uu र ू, h+ri ह ृ, h+rri ह ॄ, h+li ह ॢ we use new glyph ligature substitution
- For r+ai र ै we use kerning pair since the width of repha is very small.
- For r+i र ि we use prebase ChainingContext SingleSubstitution.
- For iVowelsign+candrabindu ि ँ, iVowelsign+anusvara ि ं, iVowelsign+repha ि र्, we use postbase ligature substitution with flags IgnoreBaseGlyphs, IgnoreLigatures.
- Anusavara Gomukha work using single substitution with new ligature glyph that has anusvaraOnGomukha. ʊ ं

किँ खिँ गिँ घिँ ङिँ चिँ छिँ जिँ झिँ ञिँ टिँ ठिँ डिँ ढिँ णिँ तिँ थिँ दिँ धिँ निँ पिँ फिँ बिँ भिँ मिँ यिँ रिँ लिँ विँ शिँ षिँ सिँ हिँ य

किँ खिँ गिँ रिँ रिं रिँ कीँ खीँ गीँ रीँ कैँ खैँ गैँ कैँ खैँ गैँ रैँ कौँ खौँ गौँ रौँ कौँ खौँ गौँ रौँ टिं टिँ रिँ रिँ रिँ किँ किँ किँ किँ

किं किँ किँ (abvm)markTomark कीँ कोँ कौँ की को कौ कीँ कोँ कौँ कें कैँ केँ कैँ केँ कैँ

In mark-to-mark, the anchor is base in one and mark in another, however both glyphs are mark glyphs in glyph properties window.

Sample Typing using Sanskrit 2020 font

अ आ इ ई उ ऊ ऋ ॠ ऌ ए ऐ ओ औ

अं आं इं ईं उं ऊं ऋं ॠं ऌं एं ऐं ओं औं

अँ आँ इँ ईँ उँ ऊँ ऋँ ॠँ ऌँ एँ ऐँ ओँ औँ

अः आः इः ईः उः ऊः ऋः ॠः ऌः एः ऐः ओः औः

ईँ ईं षँ ईं क्षँ ज्ञँ ष◌ँ ७◌ं ४◌ं ७◌ँ ७◌ं

क ख ग घ ङ च छ ज झ ञ ट ठ ड ढ ण त थ द ध न प फ ब भ म य र ल व श ष स ह
ळ ष

हरि॑ः ह॑रः ह॒रि॑ः ह॒र॑ः हरी॑ः हरि᳚ः हरि᳛ः ङ्र ट्र ठ्र ड्र ढ्र छ्र

क् ख् ग् घ् ङ् च् छ् ज् झ् ञ् ट् ठ् ड् ढ् ण् त् थ् द् ध् न् प् फ् ब् भ् म् य् र् ल् व् श् ष् स् ह्
ळ् ष◌्
कं खं गं घं ङं चं छं जं झं ञं टं ठं डं ढं णं तं थं दं धं नं पं फं बं भं मं यं रं लं वं शं षं सं हं
ळं ष◌ं
कँ खँ गँ घँ ङँ चँ छँ जँ झँ ञँ टँ ठँ डँ ढँ णँ तँ थँ दँ धँ नँ पँ फँ बँ भँ मँ यँ रँ लँ वँ शँ षँ सँ हँ
ळँ ष◌ँ
कः खः गः घः ङः चः छः जः झः ञः टः ठः डः ढः णः तः थः दः धः नः पः फः बः
भः मः यः रः लः वः शः षः सः हः ळः ष◌ः

कू॑ः खू॑ः गे॑ः घै॑ः ङो॑ः चौ॑ः छ॑ः ज॑ः झ॑ः ञ॑ः ट॑ः ठ॑ः ड॑ः ढ॑ः ण॑ः त॑ः थ॑ः द॑ः ध॑ः न॒ः प॒ः फ॒ः ब॒ः भ॒ः
म॒ः य॒ः र॒ः ल॒ः व॒ः श॒ः ष॒ः स॒ः ह॒ः ळ॒ः ष◌ः◌॒

का खा गा घा ङा चा छा जा झा ञा टा ठा डा ढा णा ता था दाधा ना पा फा बा भा मा या
रा ला वा शा षा साहाळा ष◌ा

कि खि गि घि ङि चि छि जि झि ञि टि ठि डि ढि णि ति थि दि धि नि पि फि बि भि मि यि
रि लि वि शि षि सिहिळि षि

की खी गी घी ङी ची छी जी झी ञी टी ठी डी ढी णी ती थी दी धी नी पी फी बी भी मी यी
री ली वी शी षीसीहीळी ष◌ी

कु खु गु घु ङु चु छु जु झु ञु टु ठु डु ढु णु तु थु दु धु नु पु फु बु भु मु यु रु लु वु शु षु सु हु
ळु ष◌ु
कू खू गू घू ङू चू छू जू झू ञू टू ठू डू ढू णू तू थू दू धू नू पू फू बू भू मू यू रू लू वू शू षू सू हू
ळू ष◌ू

कृ खृ गृ घृ ङृ चृ छृ जृ झृ ञृ टृ ठृ डृ ढृ णृ तृ थृ दृ धृ नृ पृ फृ बृ भृ मृ यृ रृ लृ वृ शृ षृ सृ हृ
ळृ ष◌ृ

कॄ खॄ गॄ घॄ ङॄ चॄ छॄ जॄ झॄ ञॄ टॄ ठॄ डॄ ढॄ णॄ तॄ थॄ दॄ धॄ नॄ पॄ फॄ बॄ भॄ मॄ यॄ रॄ लॄ वॄ शॄ षॄ सॄ हॄ
ळॄ ष◌ॄ

कॢ खॢ गॢ घॢ ङॢ चॢ छॢ जॢ झॢ ञॢ टॢ ठॢ डॢ ढॢ णॢ तॢ थॢ दॢ धॢ नॢ पॢ फॢ बॢ भॢ मॢ यॢ रॢ लॢ वॢ शॢ षॢ सॢ हॢ
ळॢ ष◌ॢ

के खे गे घे ङे चे छे जे झे ञे टे ठे डे ढे णे ते थे दे धे ने पे फे बे भे मे ये रे ले वे शे षे से हे
ळे ष◌े

कै खै गै घै ङै चै छै जै झै ञै टै ठै डै ढै णै तै थै दै धै नै पै फै बै भै मै यै रै लै वै शै षै सै है
ळै ष◌ै

को खो गो घो ङो चो छो जो झो ञो टो ठो डो ढो णो तो थो दो धो नो पो फो बो भो मो यो
रो लो वो शो षो सो हो ळो ष◌ो

कौ खौ गौ घौ ङौ चौ छौ जौ झौ ञौ टौ ठौ डौ ढौ णौ तौ थौ दौ धौ नौ पौ फौ बौ भौ मौ यौ
रौ लौ वौ शौ षौसौहौळौ ष◌ौ

कां खां गां घां ङां चां छां जां झां ञां टां ठां डां ढां णां तां थां दां धां नां पां फां बां भां मां यां रां लां वां शां षां सां हां ळां य

किं खिं गिं घिं ङिं चिं छिं जिं झिं ञिं टिं ठिं डिं ढिं णिं तिं थिं दिं धिं निं पिं फिं बिं भिं मिं यिं रिं लिं विं शिं षिं सिं हिं ळिं य

किँ खिँ गिँ घिँ ङिँ चिँ छिँ जिँ झिँ ञिँ टिँ ठिँ डिँ ढिँ णिँ तिँ थिँ दिँ धिँ निँ पिँ फिँ बिँ भिँ मिँ यिँ रिँ लिँ विँ शिँ षिँ सिँ हिँ ळिँ य

कीं खीं गीं घीं ङीं चीं छीं जीं झीं ञीं टीं ठीं डीं ढीं णीं तीं थीं दीं धीं नीं पीं फीं बीं भीं मीं यीं रीं लीं वीं शीं षीं सीं हीं ळीं य

कें खें गें घें ङें चें छें जें झें ञें टें ठें डें ढें णें तें थें दें धें नें पें फें बें भें में यें रें लें वें शें षें सें हें ळें य

कैं खैं गैं घैं ङैं चैं छैं जैं झैं ञैं टैं ठैं डैं ढैं णैं तैं थैं दैं धैं नैं पैं फैं बैं भैं मैं यैं रैं लैं वैं शैं षैं सैं हैं ळैं य

कों खों गों घों ङों चों छों जों झों ञों टों ठों डों ढों णों तों थों दों धों नों पों फों बों भों मों यों रों लों वों शों षों सों हों ळों य

कौं खौं गौं घौं ङौं चौं छौं जौं झौं ञौं टौं ठौं डौं ढौं णौं तौं थौं दौं धौं नौं पौं फौं बौं भौं मौं यौं रौं लौं वौं शौं षौं सौं हौं ळौं य

काँ खाँ गाँ घाँ ङाँ चाँ छाँ जाँ झाँ ञाँ टाँ ठाँ डाँ ढाँ णाँ ताँ थाँ दाँ धाँ नाँ पाँ फाँ बाँ भाँ माँ याँ राँ लाँ वाँ शाँ षाँ साँ हाँ ळाँ य

कीँ खीँ गीँ घीँ ङीँ चीँ छीँ जीँ झीँ ञीँ टीँ ठीँ डीँ ढीँ णीँ तीँ थीँ दीँ धीँ नीँ पीँ फीँ बीँ भीँ मीँ यीँ रीँ लीँ वीँ शीँ षीँ सीँ हीँ ळीँ य

केँ खेँ गेँ घेँ ङेँ चेँ छेँ जेँ झेँ ञेँ टेँ ठेँ डेँ ढेँ णेँ तेँ थेँ देँ धेँ नेँ पेँ फेँ बेँ भेँ मेँ येँ रेँ लेँ वेँ शेँ षेँ सेँ हेँ ळेँ य

कैँ खैँ गैँ घैँ ङैँ चैँ छैँ जैँ झैँ ञैँ टैँ ठैँ डैँ ढैँ णैँ तैँ थैँ दैँ धैँ नैँ पैँ फैँ बैँ भैँ मैँ यैँ रैँ लैँ वैँ शैँ षैँ सैँ हैँ
ळैँ ष

कोँ खोँ गोँ घोँ ङोँ चोँ छोँ जोँ झोँ ञोँ टोँ ठोँ डोँ ढोँ णोँ तोँ थोँ दोँ धोँ नोँ पोँ फोँ बोँ भोँ मोँ योँ
रोँ लोँ वोँ शोँ षोँ सोँ होँ ळोँ ष

कौँ खौँ गौँ घौँ ङौँ चौँ छौँ जौँ झौँ ञौँ टौँ ठौँ डौँ ढौँ णौँ तौँ थौँ दौँ धौँ नौँ पौँ फौँ बौँ भौँ मौँ यौँ
रौँ लौँ वौँ शौँ षौँ सौँ हौँ ळौँ ष

क॒ ख॒ ग॒ घ॒ ङ॒ च॒ छ॒ ज॒ झ॒ ञ॒ ट॒ ठ॒ ड॒ ढ॒ ण॒ त॒ थ॒ द॒ ध॒ न॒ प॒ फ॒ ब॒ भ॒ म॒ य॒ र॒ ल॒ व॒ श॒ ष॒ स॒ ह॒
ळ॒ ष

क॑ ख॑ ग॑ घ॑ ङ॑ च॑ छ॑ ज॑ झ॑ ञ॑ ट॑ ठ॑ ड॑ ढ॑ ण॑ त॑ थ॑ द॑ ध॑ न॑ प॑ फ॑ ब॑ भ॑ म॑ य॑ र॑ ल॑ व॑ श॑ ष॑ स॑ ह॑
ळ॑ ष

क᳚ ख᳚ ग᳚ घ᳚ ङ᳚ च᳚ छ᳚ ज᳚ झ᳚ ञ᳚ ट᳚ ठ᳚ ड᳚ ढ᳚ ण᳚ त᳚ थ᳚ द᳚ ध᳚ न᳚ प᳚ फ᳚ ब᳚ भ᳚ म᳚ य᳚ र᳚ ल᳚ व᳚ श᳚ ष᳚ स᳚ ह᳚
ळ᳚ ष

का॑ खा॑ गा॑ रा॑ कि॑ खि॑ गि॑ रि॑ की॑ खी॑ गी॑ री॑ के॑ खे॑ गे॑ रे॑ कै॑ खै॑ गै॑ रै॑ को॑ खो॑ गो॑ रो॑ कौ॑ खौ॑ गौ॑
रौ॑

का᳚ खा᳚ गा᳚ रा᳚ कि᳚ खि᳚ गि᳚ रि᳚ की᳚ खी᳚ गी᳚ री᳚ के᳚ खे᳚ गे᳚ कै᳚ खै᳚ गै᳚ रै᳚ को᳚ खो᳚ गो᳚ रो᳚ कौ᳚ खौ᳚ गौ᳚ रौ᳚

काँ खाँ गाँ राँ किँ खिँ गिँ रिँ कीँ खीँ गीँ रीँ केँ खेँ गेँ रेँ कैँ खैँ गैँ रैँ कोँ खोँ गोँ रोँ कौँ खौँ गौँ
रौँ

काँ खाँ गाँ राँ किँ खिँ गिँ रिँ कीँ खीँ गीँ रीँ केँ खेँ गेँ रेँ कैँ खैँ गैँ रैँ कोँ खोँ गोँ रोँ कौँ खौँ गौँ
रौँ

टँ टाँ टिँ टीँ टेँ टैँ टोँ टौँ कँ काँ किँ कीँ केँ कैँ कोँ कौँ सौँ

कँ काँ खाँ गाँ राँ किँ खिँ गिँ रिँ कीँ खीँ गीँ रीँ केँ खेँ गेँ रेँ कैँ खैँ गैँ रैँ कोँ खोँ गोँ रोँ कौँ खौँ
गौँ रौँ

कँ॑ काँ॑ खाँ॑ गाँ॑ राँ॑ किँ॑ खिँ॑ गिँ॑ रिँ॑ कीँ॑ खीँ॑ गीँ॑ रीँ॑ केँ॑ खेँ॑ गेँ॑ रेँ॑ कैँ॑ खैँ॑ गैँ॑ रैँ॑ कोँ॑ खोँ॑ गोँ॑ रोँ॑ कौँ॑
खौँ॑ गौँ॑ रौँ॑

कँ॑ काँ॑ खाँ॑ गाँ॑ राँ॑ किँ॑ खिँ॑ गिँ॑ रिँ॑ कीँ॑ खीँ॑ गीँ॑ रीँ॑ केँ॑ खेँ॑ गेँ॑ रेँ॑ कैँ॑ खैँ॑ गैँ॑ रैँ॑ कोँ॑ खोँ॑ गोँ॑ रोँ॑
कौँ॑ खौँ॑ गौँ॑ रौँ॑

कँ॑ काँ॑ खाँ॑ गाँ॑ राँ॑ किँ खिँ गिँ रिँ॑ कीँ॑ खीँ॑ गीँ॑ रीँ॑ केँ॑ खेँ॑ गेँ॑ रेँ॑ कैँ खैँ गैँ रैँ कोँ॑ खोँ॑ गोँ॑ रोँ॑
कौँ॑ खौँ॑ गौँ॑ रौँ॑

क᳕ ख᳖ ग᳗ घ᳘ ङ᳙ कु᳕ कू᳕ कृ᳕ कॄ᳕ कॢ᳕ कु᳖ कू᳖ कृ᳖ कॄ᳖ कॢ᳖

कु᳗ कू᳗ कृ᳗ कॄ᳗ कॢ᳗ कु᳘ कू᳘ कृ᳘ कॄ᳘ कॢ᳘ कु᳙ कू᳙ कृ᳙ कॄ᳙ कॢ᳙

क᳜ ख᳝ ग᳞ घ᳟ ङ᳜ कु᳜ कू᳜ कृ᳜ कॄ᳜ कॢ᳜

कु᳝ कू᳝ कृ᳝ कॄ᳝ कॢ᳝ कु᳝ कू᳞ कृ᳞ कॄ᳞ कॢ᳞ कु᳞ कू᳞ कृ᳞ कॄ᳞ कॢ᳞

के᳠ खे᳡ ग̄ १᳠ २᳡ ३̄

क᳜ ख᳝ ग᳞ घ᳟ ङ᳜ कु᳜ कू᳜ कृ᳜ कॄ᳜ कॢ᳜ कु᳝ कू᳝ कृ᳝ कॄ᳝ कॢ᳝

कु᳞ कू᳞ कृ᳞ कॄ᳞ कॢ᳞ कु᳟ कू᳟ कृ᳟ कॄ᳟ कॢ᳟

ख᳸ खा᳸ क᳸ का᳸ कः᳸ कं᳸ कँ᳸ क᳸ कि᳸ के᳸ कै᳸

ख᳹ खा᳹ क᳹ का᳹ कः᳹

ख̆ खा̆ क̆ का̆ कः̆ कं̆ कँ̆ क̆ कि̆ के̆ कै̆ कीं̆ कें̆ कैं̆ कों̆ कौं̆

क का कः कं कँ कं कि की के कै को कौ किं कीं कें कैं कों कौं

The glyphs 1CE2 ◌᳢ 1CE3 ◌᳣ 1CE4 ◌᳤ 1CE5 ◌᳥ 1CE6 ◌᳦ 1CE7 ◌᳧ 1CE8 ◌᳨ are for visarga only. Check their proper attachment. They should not be attachable to other consonants.

क᳢ क᳣ क᳤ क᳥ क᳦ क᳧ क᳨

कीं॑खीं॑ कैं॑ कैं᳚ कें᳚ कैं᳚ कों॑ कौं᳚ कँ॑ कँ॑ कं᳚ कँ᳚ कँ॑ कँ᳚ कँ॑ कँ॑ कँ॑ कँ॑

क॒ःकु॒ः कू॒ः कृ॒ः कः॑ कः॑ कः᳚ कᳵ॑ कᳵ᳚ क॒ᳵ कᳵ॑

काᳵ कीᳵ कूᳵ कोᳵ कृ॒ः क॒ः क्लृ॒ः कᳵ क कॢ॒ः कृ कृ॒ः क्लृ॒ः कृ किं

कीं कें कैं कौं कों किं कीं कें कैं कौं कों किं कीं कें कैं कौं कों

किं॑ कीं॑ कें॑ कैं॑ कौं॑ कों॑ किं॑ कीं॑ कें॑ कैं॑ कौं॑ कों॑ किं कीं॑ कें॑ कैं

कौं॑ कों॑ कं॑ कं॑ कं᳚ कँ॑ कँ॑ कँ॑

क॰ क॰ कॾ कॾ कॾ कॾ ७ ७ क॑ कर ७ ॐ ऐं कैं

खीं॑ खें॑ खैं॑ खों॑ खौं॑ खें॑ खं॑

कं॑ खं॑ गं॑ घं॑ ङं॑ चं॑ छं॑ जं॑ झं॑ ञं॑ टं॑ ठं॑ डं॑ ढं॑ णं॑ तं॑ थं॑ दं॑ धं॑ नं॑ पं॑ फं॑

बं॑ भं॑ मं॑ यं॑ रं॑ लं॑ वं॑ शं॑ षं॑ सं॑ हं॑

रं॑ रां॑ रिं॑ रीं॑ रुं॑ रूं॑ ऋं॑ लृं॑ ॠं॑ ॡं॑ रें॑ रैं॑ रों॑ रौं॑

खें॑ खें᳚ खें᳚ खैं॑ खैं᳚ खैं᳚ खँ॑ खँ॑ खँ᳚ खं॑ खं॑ खं᳚ खें॑ खें॑ खें᳚ खैं॑ खैं॑

खें᳚ खैं

कें॑ खें॑ गें॑ घें॑ ङें॑ चें॑ छें॑ जें॑ झें॑ ञें॑ टें॑ ठें॑ डें॑ ढें॑ णें॑ तें॑ थें॑ दें॑ धें॑ नें॑ पें॑ फें॑

बें॑ भें॑ में॑ यें॑ रें॑ लें॑ वें॑ शें॑ षें॑ सें॑ हें॑

के᳚ खे᳚ गे᳚ घे᳚ ङे᳚ चे᳚ छे᳚ जे᳚ झे᳚ ञे᳚ टे᳚ ठे᳚ डे᳚ ढे᳚ णे᳚ ते᳚ थे᳚ दे᳚ धे᳚ ने᳚ पे᳚ फे᳚
बे᳚ भे᳚ मे᳚ ये᳚ रे᳚ ले᳚ वे᳚ शे᳚ षे᳚ से᳚ हे᳚

के᳛ खे᳛ गे᳛ घे᳛ ङे᳛ चे᳛ छे᳛ जे᳛ झे᳛ ञे᳛ टे᳛ ठे᳛ डे᳛ ढे᳛ णे᳛ ते᳛ थे᳛ दे᳛ धे᳛ ने᳛ पे᳛
फे᳛ बे᳛ भे᳛ मे᳛ ये᳛ रे᳛ ले᳛ वे᳛ शे᳛ षे᳛ से᳛ हे᳛

कै॑ खै॑ गै॑ घै॑ ङै॑ चै॑ छै॑ जै॑ झै॑ ञै॑ टै॑ ठै॑ डै॑ ढै॑ णै॑ तै॑ थै॑ दै॑ धै॑ नै॑ पै॑ फै॑
बै॑ भै॑ मै॑ यै॑ रै॑ लै॑ वै॑ शै॑ षै॑ सै॑ है॑
कै᳚ खै᳚ गै᳚ घै᳚ ङै᳚ चै᳚ छै᳚ जै᳚ झै᳚ ञै᳚ टै᳚ ठै᳚ डै᳚ ढै᳚ णै᳚ तै᳚ थै᳚ दै᳚ धै᳚ नै᳚ पै᳚
फै᳚ बै᳚ भै᳚ मै᳚ यै᳚ रै᳚ लै᳚ वै᳚ शै᳚ षै᳚ सै᳚ है᳚

कै᳛ खै᳛ गै᳛ घै᳛ ङै᳛ चै᳛ छै᳛ जै᳛ झै᳛ ञै᳛ टै᳛ ठै᳛ डै᳛ ढै᳛ णै᳛ तै᳛ थै᳛ दै᳛
धै᳛ नै᳛ पै᳛ फै᳛ बै᳛ भै᳛ मै᳛ यै᳛ रै᳛ लै᳛ वै᳛ शै᳛ षै᳛ सै᳛ है᳛

को॑ खो॑ गो॑ घो॑ ङो॑ चो॑ छो॑ जो॑ झो॑ ञो॑ टो॑ ठो॑ डो॑ ढो॑ णो॑ तो॑ थो॑
दो॑ धो॑ नो॑ पो॑ फो॑ बो॑ भो॑ मो॑ यो॑ रो॑ लो॑ वो॑ शो॑ षो॑ सो॑ हो॑

को᳚ खो᳚ गो᳚ घो᳚ ङो᳚ चो᳚ छो᳚ जो᳚ झो᳚ ञो᳚ टो᳚ ठो᳚ डो᳚ ढो᳚ णो᳚ तो᳚ थो᳚
दो᳚ धो᳚ नो᳚ पो᳚ फो᳚ बो᳚ भो᳚ मो᳚ यो᳚ रो᳚ लो᳚ वो᳚ शो᳚ षो᳚ सो᳚ हो᳚

कौ खौ गौ घौ ङौ चौ छौ जौ झौ ञौ टौ ठौ डौ ढौ णौ तौ थौ
दौ धौ नौ पौ फौ बौ भौ मौ यौ रौ लौ वौ शौ षौ सौ हौ
कौ खौ गौ घौ ङौ चौ छौ जौ झौ ञौ टौ ठौ डौ ढौ णौ तौ थौ
दौ धौ नौ पौ फौ बौ भौ मौ यौ रौ लौ वौ शौ षौ सौ हौ
कौ खौ गौ घौ ङौ चौ छौ जौ झौ ञौ टौ ठौ डौ ढौ णौ तौ
थौ दौ धौ नौ पौ फौ बौ भौ मौ यौ रौ लौ वौ शौ षौ सौ हौ
कौ खौ गौ घौ ङौ चौ छौ जौ झौ ञौ टौ ठौ डौ ढौ णौ तौ थौ
दौ धौ नौ पौ फौ बौ भौ मौ यौ रौ लौ वौ शौ षौ सौ हौ

की खी गी घी ङी ची छी जी झी ञी टी ठी डी ढी णी ती थी
दी धी नी पी फी बी भी मी यी री ली वी शी षी सी ही

की खी गी घी ङी ची छी जी झी ञी टी ठी डी ढी णी ती थी
दी धी नी पी फी बी भी मी यी री ली वी शी षी सी ही

की खी गी घी ङी ची छी जी झी ञी टी ठी डी ढी णी ती थी
दी धी नी पी फी बी भी मी यी री ली वी शी षी सी ही

कं॑ खं॑ गं॑ घं॑ ङं॑ चं॑ छं॑ जं॑ झं॑ ञं॑ टं॑ ठं॑ डं॑ ढं॑ णं॑ तं॑ थं॑ दं॑ धं॑ नं॑ पं॑ फं॑
बं॑ भं॑ मं॑ यं॑ रं॑ लं॑ वं॑ शं॑ षं॑ सं॑ हं॑
कं᳚ खं᳚ गं᳚ घं᳚ ङं᳚ चं᳚ छं᳚ जं᳚ झं᳚ ञं᳚ टं᳚ ठं᳚ डं᳚ ढं᳚ णं᳚ तं᳚ थं᳚ दं᳚ धं᳚ नं᳚ पं᳚ फं᳚
बं᳚ भं᳚ मं᳚ यं᳚ रं᳚ लं᳚ वं᳚ शं᳚ षं᳚ सं᳚ हं᳚

कं᳛ खं᳛ गं᳛ घं᳛ ङं᳛ चं᳛ छं᳛ जं᳛ झं᳛ ञं᳛ टं᳛ ठं᳛ डं᳛ ढं᳛ णं᳛ तं᳛ थं᳛ दं᳛ धं᳛ नं᳛ पं᳛ फं᳛
बं᳛ भं᳛ मं᳛ यं᳛ रं᳛ लं᳛ वं᳛ शं᳛ षं᳛ सं᳛ हं᳛
कँ॑ खँ॑ गँ॑ घँ॑ ङँ॑ चँ॑ छँ॑ जँ॑ झँ॑ ञँ॑ टँ॑ ठँ॑ डँ॑ ढँ॑ णँ॑ तँ॑ थँ॑ दँ॑ धँ॑ नँ॑ पँ॑ फँ॑
बँ॑ भँ॑ मँ॑ यँ॑ रँ॑ लँ॑ वँ॑ शँ॑ षँ॑ सँ॑ हँ॑

कँ᳚ खँ᳚ गँ᳚ घँ᳚ ङँ᳚ चँ᳚ छँ᳚ जँ᳚ झँ᳚ ञँ᳚ टँ᳚ ठँ᳚ डँ᳚ ढँ᳚ णँ᳚ तँ᳚ थँ᳚ दँ᳚ धँ᳚ नँ᳚ पँ᳚
फँ᳚ बँ᳚ भँ᳚ मँ᳚ यँ᳚ रँ᳚ लँ᳚ वँ᳚ शँ᳚ षँ᳚ सँ᳚ हँ᳚

कँ᳛ खँ᳛ गँ᳛ घँ᳛ ङँ᳛ चँ᳛ छँ᳛ जँ᳛ झँ᳛ ञँ᳛ टँ᳛ ठँ᳛ डँ᳛ ढँ᳛ णँ᳛ तँ᳛ थँ᳛ दँ᳛ धँ᳛
नँ᳛ पँ᳛ फँ᳛ बँ᳛ भँ᳛ मँ᳛ यँ᳛ रँ᳛ लँ᳛ वँ᳛ शँ᳛ षँ᳛ सँ᳛ हँ᳛

(double and triple svarita occupy space above turban of the following varna also and may obstruct their matra.) Use ligature substitution.

कं॑ खं॑ गं॑ घं॑ ङं॑ चं॑ छं॑ जं॑ झं॑ ञं॑ टं॑ ठं॑ डं॑ ढं॑ णं॑ तं॑ थं॑ दं॑ धं॑ नं॑ पं॑ फं॑
बं॑ भं॑ मं॑ यं॑ रं॑ लं॑ वं॑ शं॑ षं॑ सं॑ हं॑

कं॥ खं॥ गं॥ घं॥ ङं॥ चं॥ छं॥ जं॥ झं॥ ञं॥ टं॥ ठं॥ डं॥ ढं॥ णं॥ तं॥ थं॥ दं॥ धं॥ नं॥ पं॥ फं॥
बं॥ भं॥ मं॥ यं॥ रं॥ लं॥ वं॥ शं॥ षं॥ सं॥ हं॥

कं॥। खं॥। गं॥। घं॥। ङं॥। चं॥। छं॥। जं॥। झं॥। ञं॥। टं॥। ठं॥। डं॥। ढं॥। णं॥। तं॥। थं॥। दं॥। धं॥। नं॥। पं॥।
फं॥। बं॥। भं॥। मं॥। यं॥। रं॥। लं॥। वं॥। शं॥। षं॥। सं॥। हं॥।

कं। खं। गं। घं। ङं। चं। छं। जं। झं। ञं। टं। ठं। डं। ढं। णं। तं। थं। दं। धं। नं। पं। फं।
बं। भं। मं। यं। रं। लं। वं। शं। षं। सं। हं।

कं। खं। गं। घं। ङं। चं। छं। जं। झं। ञं। टं। ठं। डं। ढं। णं। तं। थं। दं। धं। नं। पं। फं।
बं। भं। मं। यं। रं। लं। वं। शं। षं। सं। हं।

कँ॥। खँ॥। गँ॥। घँ॥। ङँ॥। चँ॥। छँ॥। जँ॥। झँ॥। ञँ॥। टँ॥। ठँ॥। डँ॥। ढँ॥। णँ॥। तँ॥। थँ॥। दँ॥।
धँ॥। नँ॥। पँ॥। फँ॥। बँ॥। भँ॥। मँ॥। यँ॥। रँ॥। लँ॥। वँ॥। शँ॥। षँ॥। सँ॥। हँ॥।

कँ। खँ। गँ। घँ। ङँ। चँ। छँ। जँ। झँ। ञँ। टँ। ठँ। डँ। ढँ। णँ। तँ। थँ। दँ। धँ। नँ।
पँ। फँ। बँ। भँ। मँ। यँ। रँ। लँ। वँ। शँ। षँ। सँ। हँ।

कँ॥ खँ॥ गँ॥ घँ॥ ङँ॥ चँ॥ छँ॥ जँ॥ झँ॥ ञँ॥ टँ॥ ठँ॥ डँ॥ ढँ॥ णँ॥ तँ॥ थँ॥ दँ॥
धँ॥ नँ॥ पँ॥ फँ॥ बँ॥ भँ॥ मँ॥

यँ॥ रँ॥ here left and right kern spacing is to be corrected in the glyph.
लँ॥ वँ॥

Check the right side bearing for these glyphs.

कँ खँ गँ घँ ङँ चँ छँ जँ झँ ञँ टँ ठँ डँ ढँ णँ तँ

थँ दँ धँ नँ पँ फँ बँ भँ मँ यँ रँ लँ वँ शँ षँ सँ हँ

ऐं ईं औं ओं ऐं ईं औं ओं ऐं ईं औं ओं ऐं ईं औं ओं

Check and correct

औँ ओँ ऐँ ईँ औं ओं कां नां कँ

ऐँ ईँ औँ ओँ ऐँ ईँ औँ ओँ ऐँ ऐँ ईँ

ईँ औँ औँ ओँ

Positioning 4 or more glyphs

Positioning 4 glyphs is a challenge. ह ि◌ ◌ः ◌॑

(base+matra+visarga+svarita $0951).

The svarita $0951 always intersects. We need to position it a bit to the right so that it does not intersect the top matra. It should get positioned similar to anudatta $0952. E.g.

हरि॒ः   हरी॒ः हरे॒ः हरै॒ः हरो॒ः हरौ॒ः

(note: svarita is called udatta in unicode).

We achieved it using a composite ligature substitution!

हरि॑ः   हरी॑ः हरे॑ः   हरै॑ः हरो॑ः हरौ॑ः

Use Composite glyph rather than combining

If a composite glyph is available, use it instead of combining two or more independent glyphs from the character sets.

Challenges of incorrect ligatures

Svarita Accent Placement with Top Repha

- र्ध॑ र्क॑ र्ड॑ र्ख॑ र्क॑
- र्घ॑ र्क॑ र्ड॑ र्ख॑ र्क॑ र्ग॑ र्घ॑ र्ल॑ पुष्टिवर्ध॑नम्
- क का कि की कु कू कृ कॢ के कै को कौ कं कः ।
- क॑ का॑ कि॑ की॑ कु॑ कू॑ कृ॑ कॢ॑ के॑ कै॑ को॑ कौ॑ कं॑ कः॑ । size of bottom vocalic li matra is huge.
- क॑ का॑ कि॑ की॑ कु॑ कू॑ कृ॑ कॢ॑ के॑ कै॑ को॑ कौ॑ कं॑ कः॑ ।
- क का कि की कु कू कृ कॢ के कै को कौ कं कः ।

Svarita Accent with Anusvara

- अं आं इं ईं उं ऊं ऋं ॠं ऌं एं ऐं ओं औं
- अं॑ आं॑ इं॑ (ईं॑) उं॑ ऊं॑ ऋं॑ ॠं॑ ऌं॑ एं॑ ऐं॑ ओं॑ औं॑
- अं॑ आं॑ इं॑ (ईं॑) उं॑ ऊं॑ ऋं॑ ॠं॑ ऌं॑ एं॑ ऐं॑ ओं॑ औं॑

कं॑ कं॑ किं॑ किं॑ कीं॑ कैं॑ कैं॑ कीं॑   कं॑ कं॑ किं॑ कीं॑ कैं॑ कैं॑

Anudatta Accent with Visarga

अः॒ अ॒᳚ आᳵ इ ई उ ऊ ऋ ॠ ऌ ए ऐ ओ औ अं अः अᳵ

अ॒ आ॒ इ॒ ई॒ उ॒ ऊ॒ ऋ॒ ॠ॒ ऌ॒ ए॒ ऐ॒ ओ॒ औ॒ अं॒ अः॒ anudatta here got shifted correctly due to markTomark positioning!

अः॒ आः॒ इः॒ ईः॒ उः॒ ऊः॒ ऋः॒ ॠः॒ ऌः॒ एः॒ ऐः॒ ओः॒ औः॒ अं॒

क कृ को की कः खः

Anudatta Accent with Bottom Matra/Conjunct

Classic example of incorrect Anudatta Accent placement with Bottom matra in common fonts.

Sanskrit 2003 युप कृ and Sanskrit 2020 ok युप कृ

Arial Unicode युप कृ

Sakal Bharati युप कृ

CDAC Dhruv युप कृ

Annapurna SIL युप कृ

Adishila युप कृ and Siddhanta ok युप कृ

Dirgha Svarita Accent Placement with TOP Matra

Classic example of incorrect Dirgha Svarita Accent placement.
NA = Not Available. NAU= Not Available in correct unicode space

Sanskrit 2003 कै NAU

Arial Unicode कै NA

CDAC Dhruv कै NA

Annapurna SIL कै NA

Adishila touches the matra कै᳚ कि᳚ की᳚

Siddhanta is fine कै᳚ कि᳚ की᳚

Added unicode block Vedic Extensions. Dirgha svarita Glyph 1CDA Copied glyph from Private Use Area glyph E008 to 1CDA.
Note – in word 2019 it shows as Buginese Unicode Block. Perhaps Vedic Extensions was not implemented completely in MS Word 2019 version.

Sanskrit 2020 कै᳚ कि᳚ की᳚

क का कि की कु कू कृ कॢ के कै को कौ कं कः

devanagaristresssignudattacomb

क॑ का॑ कि॑ की॑ कु॑ कू॑ कृ॑ कॢ॑ के॑ कै॑ को॑ कौ॑ कं॑ कः॑

vedictonedoublesvaritacomb

क᳚ का᳚ कि᳚ की᳚ कु᳚ कू᳚ कृ᳚ कॢ᳚ के᳚ कै᳚ को᳚ कौ᳚ कं᳚ कः᳚

क᳚ का᳚ कि᳚ की᳚ कु᳚ कू᳚ कृ᳚ कॢ᳚ के᳚ कै᳚ को᳚ कौ᳚ कं᳚ कः᳚

क᳚ का᳚ कि᳚ की᳚ कु᳚ कू᳚ कृ᳚ कॢ᳚ के᳚ कै᳚ को᳚ कौ᳚ कं᳚ कः᳚

Samaveda Accents ‘Add Space Before/After Paragraph’

For visibility of the typed tones in Samaveda, we need to use correct paragraph spacing.

अ आ इ ई ऐ औ अ आ इ ई ऐ औ अ आ इ
ई ऐ औ ई ऐ औ Check and correct

अग्नआ याहि वीतये गृणानोहव्यदातये ।

नि होता सत्सि बर्हिषि ॥ १ ॥

ओग्ना इ । आयाही३ वीइया२◌इ ।

आनोविश्वासुहव्यमिन्द्रꣳसमत्सुभूषत ।

We have positioned accents above WinAscent, or below WinDescent, for proper size readability. Hence in a text editor like MS Word, it is needed to use ‘Add Space Before Paragraph’ or ‘Add Space After Paragraph’ for these to render correctly.

Changes needed in the shaping engine

Gomukha Anusvara U+1CE9

Changes needed in the shaping engine in Open Type design, somewhere in the back-end of code or the implementation in MS Word editor. Gomukha Anusvaras are blocked from combining with Anusvara and Candrabindu.

ᳩ◌ं ᳩ◌ँ should be actually ᳩं ᳪं ᳫं ᳬं ᳮं ᳩँ ᳪँ ᳫँ ᳬँ ᳮँ

Work around to implement them in a Devanagari font for now. Simply insert new characters in Private Use Area, and draw the correct ligatures. Then we can use Insert-Symbol in a Word Editor to type these.

Heavy yya U+097A

ॺ◌् ॺ◌ा ॺ◌्ॺ ॺ◌ा ॺ◌ु ॺ॑

glyph U+097A, how to attach to Vowel sign?
Always shows vowel sign with dotted circle. Perhaps hardcoded in shaping engine back-end.

ॺ ॺा ॺी ॺू workaround.

Ardhavisarga U+1CF2

This symbol is not available in Sanskrit2003 font, and is available in updated Sanskrit 2020 font.

- Added ardhavisarga glyph 1CF2 in unicode block Vedic Extensions.
- Copied visarga 0903 to ardhavisarga glyph 1CF2.
- Copied candrabindu 0901 into 1CF2 and modified it to ardhavisarga.
- कᳲ अᳲ अः कः

- In glyph 1CF2 Anchor_4 already copied. We simply add code for anudatta. belowbasemarkpositioning-marktobase
- However it does not attach to Vowels or Consonants. Perhaps hardcoded. Work around.

Numeral १ and ३ Accents

१◌॑◌॒ ३◌॑◌॒ both accents needed simultaneously for these two numerals.

१॒॑ ३॒॑ Work around by new ligatures in Private Use Area.

Numeral २ Tones U+1CD0

२᳐ २᳑ २᳒ these tones are only for the numeral २. Not to be used for any other Letter or Vowel or Consonant.

https://www.unicode.org/Public/13.0.0/ucd/IndicSyllabicCategory.txt
https://www.unicode.org/L2/L2021/21006-gomukha.pdf
https://docs.microsoft.com/en-us/typography/script-development/use
https://docs.microsoft.com/en-us/typography/script-development/devanagari

ख् खा ऽख खा खु ख॑, ०ं ०ं ०ँ ०ँ ०॑, १॒॑ ३॒॑, २᳐ २᳑ २᳒

Accents for Candrabindu Virama U+A8F3

To implement anudatta and svarita for ꣳ॒ Workaround by making new ligatures in Private Use Area.

ꣳ ꣳ॑ꣳ᳚ꣳ॒

ꣴ ꣴ॒ꣴ॑ꣴ᳚

[illegible] [illegible]

Nasalized semivowel

Maha Mrityunjaye Mantra Usually written as

त्र्य॑म्बकꣳ यजामहे सुग॑न्धिं पु॑ष्टिवर्ध॑नम् ।
उर्वा॑रुकमि॑व बन्ध॑नान् मृ॒त्योर् मु॑क्षीय माऽमृता᳚त् ॥

For teaching Sanskrit Grammar and pronunciation we will use Nasalized semivowel.

त्र्य॑म्बकयँ॒ यजामहे सुग॑न्धिं पु॑ष्टिवर्ध॑नम् ।
उर्वा॑रुकमि॑व बन्ध॑नान् मृ॒त्योर् मु॑क्षीय माऽमृता᳚त् ॥

Indic Shaping and Spell Check Requirements

Listing our understanding regarding Indic Shaping Requirements to prevent invalid Sanskrit word formation. Our Proposals regarding Sanskrit spell check or correct shaping engine coding. These are listed after a careful study of Sanskrit Literature, including Classical and Vedic, Rigveda, Samaveda, Shukla Yajurveda, Krishna Yajurveda, Atharvaveda. This section has been given because the harfbuzz shaping engine allows any combination of letters. That is a serious error in implementation. It must be avoided.

https://typedrawers.com/discussion/3870/attaching-a-devanagari-vedic-extensions-base-glyph-with-a-mark

Consider the Devanagari Unicode Block U+0900 to 097F = 128 glyphs.

From a purely Sanskrit Language point-of-view (wherein glyphs from Awadhi, Dravidian, etc. are not accounted for).

The characters herein are classified as:

- Base Glyph Vowel = U+0905 to 090C, 090F, 0910, 0913, 0914, 0960, 0961= 14 glyphs = **V**
- Base Glyph Consonant = U+0915 to 0928, 092A to 0930, 0932, 0933, 0935 to 0939, 097A = 35 glyphs = **C**
- Mark Glyph Matra Vowel Sign = U+093E to 0944, 0947, 0948, 094B, 094C, 0962, 0963 = 13 glyphs = **M**
- Mark Glyph Nasalization and Aspirate Signs = U+0900, 0901, 0902, 0903 = 4 glyphs = **N**
- Mark Glyph Accent Stress Sign = U+0951, 0952 = 2 glyphs = **A**

- Numerals = U+0966 to 0970 = 10 glyphs = **D**
- Punctuation Sign = U+0964, 0965 = 2 glyphs = **P**
- Sandhi Sign = U+093D = 1 glyph = **S**
- Halant Virama Sign = U+094D = 1 glyph = **H**

For the purposes of this discussion we have given arbitrary abbreviations:

V = Base Glyph Vowel

C = Base Glyph Consonant

M = Mark Glyph Matra Vowel Sign

N = Mark Glyph Nasalization and Aspirate Sign

A = Mark Glyph Accent Stress Sign

Indic Shaping properties must account for the following to create VALID SANSKRIT TEXT:

1. Base Glyph Vowel = **V should not attach** to Mark Glyph Matra Vowel Sign = **M.**
"VM" is an invalid combination. Indic shaping must prevent this.

e.g. U+0905+0940 is invalid. अी INVALID SANSKRIT.

2. Base Glyph Vowel = **V can attach** to **only one glyph** from the - Mark Glyph Nasalization and Aspirate Signs = **N**
"VNN" is an invalid combination. Here the last typed glyph should erase any previous **N**.
e.g. U+0905+0901+0903 is invalid. 0905+0901+0901 is invalid.

अंः INVALID SANSKRIT.

3. Base Glyph Vowel = **V can attach** to **only one glyph** from the - Mark Glyph Accent Stress Sign = **A**
"VAA" is an invalid combination. Here the last typed glyph should erase any previous **A**.
e.g. U+0905+0951+0952 is invalid. 0905+0951+0951 is invalid.

अ॒॑ INVALID SANSKRIT.

4. Base Glyph Vowel = **V can attach** to **only two glyphs** from glyph sets (**N, A**) with the provision that the two glyphs are from distinct glyph sets.

"VNA", "VAN" are valid combinations.

E.g. **U+0905+0901+0952 is valid.**

अँ॒ VALID.

"VNAN", "VANA" are invalid. Here the last typed glyph should erase any previous **N, A if duplicate**.

अँ॒ँ INVALID SANSKRIT.

अँ॒ः INVALID SANSKRIT.

5a. Ligatures consisting of Punctuation Sign **P** must be **prevented** in Indic shaping.

E.g. **U+0964+0901 is invalid. U+0965+0903 is invalid.**

।ँ INVALID SANSKRIT.

॥ः INVALID SANSKRIT. (correctly implemented in harfbuzz!)

5a. Ligatures consisting of Sandhi Sign **S** must be **prevented** in Indic shaping.

E.g. **U+093D+0902 is invalid. U+093D+0903 is invalid.**

ऽं INVALID SANSKRIT. (correctly implemented in harfbuzz!)

ऽः INVALID SANSKRIT.

ऽ् INVALID SANSKRIT.

6. Ligatures consisting **only** of Numerals १ or ३ along with **both** the Accent signs **A** simultaneously are permitted. A single accent sign with these numerals is INVALID.

U+0967 + 0951 + 0952 (all three together) is valid. १॒॑ **VALID.**

U+0969 + 0951 + 0952 (all three together) is valid. ३॒॑ **VALID.**

U+0967 + 0951 is invalid. १॑ **INVALID SANSKRIT.**

U+0967 + 0952 is invalid. १॒ **INVALID SANSKRIT.**

U+0969 + 0951 is invalid. ३॑ **INVALID SANSKRIT.**

U+0969 + 0952 is invalid. ३॒ **INVALID SANSKRIT.**

7. Base Glyph Consonant = **C can attach** to **only one** Mark Glyph Matra Vowel Sign = **M.**
"CM" is a valid combination.
"CMM" is invalid. Indic shaping must prevent this by keeping only the last typed **M**.
E.g. **U+0915+093E+0940 is invalid.**

काी **INVALID SANSKRIT.**

कीू **INVALID SANSKRIT.**

8. Base Glyph Consonant = **C can attach** to **only three total glyphs** from glyph sets (**M**, **N, A**) with the provision that the three glyphs are from distinct glyph sets, and **CM** cluster precedes the others.
"CMNA", "CMAN", "CNA", "CAN" are valid combinations.
"CMNAN", "CMANA" are invalid. Here the last typed glyph should erase any previous **N, A if duplicate**.
E.g. **U+0915+093E+0902+0940+903 is invalid.**

कांीः **INVALID SANSKRIT.**

9. With the use of Halant Virama Sign **H,** indic shaping must **select the appropriate consonant ligatures** if present in the font.

10. For **invalid** combinations, the dotted circle glyph 25CC **must show** if implemented in font. Or, such an invalid combination must not be typable at all!
e.g.

1. अ◌ी

2. अं◌ः

3. अ॑◌॒

4. अं॒◌ः

5a. ।◌ँ ॥◌ः 5b. ऽ◌ं ऽ◌ी

6. १◌॑ ३◌॒

7. का◌ी

8. का॒ः◌ं

Shaping Technical Terms in Unicode

Mark having Indic Shaping class = **None**
Devanagari Block **Independent Mark**

- Om = Sacred symbol

Diacritics having Indic Shaping class = **Bindu**
Devanagari Block **Dependent NonSpacing Mark**

- CANDRABINDU, ANUSVARA = nazalization mark

Diacritic having Indic Shaping class = **Visarga**
Devanagari Block **Dependent Spacing Mark**

- VISARGA = air exhalation mark, subclass = Right Position

Diacritics having Indic Shaping class = **Cantillation**
Devanagari Block **Dependent NonSpacing Mark**

- Svarita = high pitch accent, subclass = Top Position
- Anudatta = low pitch accent, subclass = Bottom Position

Diacritic having Indic Shaping class = **Nukta**
Devanagari Block **Dependent NonSpacing Mark**

- NUKTA = tongue placement mark, subclass = Bottom Position

Diacritic having Indic Shaping class = **Virama**
Devanagari Block **Dependent NonSpacing Mark**

- HALANT=consonant vowel removal,subclass=Bottom Position

Letter having Indic Shaping class = **Avagraha**
Devanagari Block **Independent Letter**

- AVAGRAHA = indicates a dropped अ vowel

Punctuations having Indic Shaping class = **None**
Devanagari Block **Independent Punctuation**

- Danda = indicates a stop or pause in a verse
- Double Danda = indicates a full stop.
- Abbreviation Ring = indicates an abbreviated word.

Letters having Indic Shaping class = **Consonant**
Devanagari Block **Independent Letter**

- Consonant क ख ग घ ङ च छ ज झ ञ ट ठ ड ढ ण त थ द ध न प फ ब भ म य र ल व श ष स ह ळ य

Letters having Indic Shaping class = **Vowel**
Devanagari Block **Independent Letter**

- Vowels अ आ इ ई उ ऊ ऋ ॠ ऌ ॡ ए ऐ ओ औ

Marks having Indic Shaping class = **Vowel Matra**
Devanagari Block **Dependent Mark**

- Matras ◌ा ◌ि ◌ी ◌ु ◌ू ◌ृ ◌ॄ ◌ॢ ◌ॣ ◌े ◌ै ◌ो ◌ौ

Vowel Matra subclass = **Matra Position**

- **Spacing** Matra Position Left = Prebase ◌ि
- **Spacing** Matra Position Right = Postbase ◌ा ◌ी ◌ो ◌ौ
- **NonSpacing** Matra Position Top = Abovebase ◌े ◌ै
- **NonSpacing** Matra Bottom = Belowbase ◌ु ◌ू ◌ृ ◌ॄ ◌ॢ ◌ॣ

Numbers having Indic Shaping class = **Number**
Devanagari Block **Independent Number**

- Numbers १ २ ३ ४ ५ ६ ७ ८ ९ ०

Note:

Numbers १ २ ३ should have a special shaping class. This is so that the Vedic Tones U+1CD0, 1CD1, 1CD2 can get attached above to these numerals alone, and not to any other Letter, Vowel or Consonant.

१᳐ २᳑ ३᳒

Numbers १ ३ should have a special shaping class. This is so that the Vedic Accents Svarita U+0951, Anudatta U+0952, can **both** get attached **simultaneously** to these numerals alone. For other Letters, Vowels or Consonants, **only one accent** can get attached at a time.

Symbols having Indic Shaping class = **Special Function**
Geometric Shapes Block

- Dotted circle ◌ U+25CC = to show a missing base glyph
- No-break Space U+00A0 = to prevent dotted cirle
- Zero Width Non-Joiner U+200C = to prevent conjunct glyph
- Zero Width Joiner U+200D = to prevent half-forms glyph

Vedic Tone Marks having Indic Shaping class = **Cantillation**
Vedic Extensions Block **Dependent NonSpacing Mark**

- U+1CD0 – 1CD2 = attach above cantillation marks
- U+1CD5 – 1CD9 = attach below cantillation marks
- U+1CDA – 1CDB = attach above cantillation marks
- U+1CDC – 1CDF = attach below cantillation marks
- U+1CE0 = attach above cantillation mark
- U+1CF4 = attach above cantillation mark
- U+1CF8 – 1CF9 = attach above cantillation marks

Vedic Punctuations having Indic Shaping class = **None**
Vedic Extensions Block **Independent Punctuation**

- U+1CD3 = independent symbol

Vedic Mark having Indic Shaping class = **Cantillation**
Vedic Extensions Block **Dependent Mark**

- U+1CD4 = special svarita

Vedic Mark having Indic Shaping class = **Cantillation**
Vedic Extensions Block **Independent Spacing Mark**

- U+1CE1 = independent svarita

Vedic Marks having Indic Shaping class = **Avagraha**
Vedic Extensions Block Dependent Mark

- U+1CE2 – 1CE8 = attach to visarga

Vedic Other Letters having Indic Shaping class = **Symbol**
Vedic Extensions Block **Independent Other Letter**

- U+1CE9 – 1CEC = independent gomukha anusvara symbols, *should be like base glyphs for Bindu to get attached.*

Vedic Marks having Indic Shaping class = **Avagraha**
Vedic Extensions Block **Dependent Mark**

- U+1CED = tiryak that attachs below gomukha anusvaras

Vedic Other Letters having Indic Shaping class = **Symbol**
Vedic Extensions Block **Independent Other Letter**

- U+1CEE – 1CF1 = independent long anusvara symbols

Vedic Letters having Indic Shaping class = **Consonant_Dead**
Vedic Extensions Block **Independent Other Letter**

- U+1CF2 – 1CF3 = ardhavisarga, *should be dependent marks*

Vedic Mark having Indic Shaping class = **None**
Vedic Extensions Block **Independent Spacing Mark**

- U+1CF7 = atikrama symbol

Vedic Other Letter having Indic Shaping class = **Symbol**
Vedic Extensions Block **Independent Other Letter**

- U+1CFA = independent double gomukha anusvara symbol

Vedic Marks having Indic Shaping class = **Cantillation**
Devanagari Extended Block **Dependent NonSpacing Mark**

- U+A8E0 – A8E9 = combining numerals, position top
- U+A8EA – A8F0 = combining letters, position top
- U+A8F1 = combining avagraha, position top

Vedic Letters having Indic Shaping class = **Symbol**
Devanagari Extended Block **Independent Other Letter**

- U+A8F2 – A8F7 = long candrabindu symbols

Vedic Punctuations having Indic Shaping class = **None**
Devanagari Extended Block **Other Punctuation Mark**

- U+A8F8 – A8FA = vedic punctuations, independent symbols
- U+A8FC = vedic sacred symbol, independent symbol

Vedic Symbol having Indic Shaping class = **None**
Devanagari Extended Block **Other Letter Symbols**

- U+A8FB = vedic symbol, independent symbol

Vedic Symbol having Indic Shaping class = **None**
Devanagari Extended Block **Other Letter Symbols**

- U+A8FD = jain sacred symbol, independent symbol

Vedic Letter having Indic Shaping class = **Vowel**
Devanagari Extended Block **Independent Other Letter**

- U+A8FE = vowel symbol, independent symbol

Vedic Mark having Indic Shaping class = **Vowel Matra**
Devanagari Extended Block **Dependent NonSpacing Mark**

- U+A8FF = combining vowel matra

References

https://www.ashtangayoga.info/philosophy/sanskrit-and-devanagari/transliteration-tool/
https://www.learnsanskrit.cc/
https://scriptsource.org/
https://scriptsource.org/cms/scripts/page.php?item_id=wrSys_detail&key=sa-Deva
https://scriptsource.org/cms/scripts/page.php?item_id=language_detail_font&key=san
https://scriptsource.org/cms/scripts/page.php?item_id=script_detail&key=Deva

Latin Transliteration
https://en.wikipedia.org/wiki/International_Alphabet_of_Sanskrit_Transliteration
https://scriptsource.org/cms/scripts/page.php?item_id=entry_detail&uid=g8w4snzcy5
https://cdn.standards.iteh.ai/samples/28333/a0a778b7b2034a91aab1e97b3a34d125/ISO-15919-2001.pdf
https://www.lexilogos.com/keyboard/sanskrit_conversion.htm

Unicode Standard Version 4.0 dated Aug 2003
https://www.unicode.org/versions/Unicode4.0.0/ch09.pdf

Unicode Standard Version 13.0 dated Mar 2020
Chapter 12 South and Central Asia-I Official Scripts of India
https://www.unicode.org/versions/Unicode13.0.0/ch12.pdf

Unicode Standard Version 14.0 dated Sept 2021
https://www.unicode.org/versions/Unicode14.0.0/ch12.pdf

Unicode Standard Version 15.0 dated Sept 2022
https://www.unicode.org/versions/Unicode15.0.0/ch12.pdf

Sanskrit Devanagari Font List
https://list.indology.info/pipermail/indology/attachments/20230805/cdea9f08/attachment.htm

Font Sanskrit 2020
https://sourceforge.net/projects/advaita-sharada-font/files/Devanagari/

Font Sanskrit 2003 https://www.oah.in/Sanskrit/itranslator2003.htm
https://www.oah.in/Sanskrit/Sanskrit2003_30.07.2019.zip
Font Annapurna SIL https://software.sil.org/annapurna/
Font Arial Unicode MS https://www.download-free-fonts.com/details/88978/arial-unicode-ms
Font Lohit Devanagari
https://github.com/google/fonts/blob/master/ofl/lohitdevanagari/Lohit-Devanagari.ttf
Font CDAC Dhruv, Yogesh, Sakal Bharati
https://www.cdac.in/index.aspx?id=dl_sakal_bharati_font
Font Siddhanta http://svayambhava.blogspot.com/p/siddhanta-devanagariunicode-open-type.html
Font Chandas Uttara http://www.sanskritweb.net/cakram/
Google Noto https://fonts.google.com/noto/fonts?noto.query=dev
Font Adishila https://adishila.com/fonts/
Font Shobhika https://www.kramasubramanian.com/resources/shobhika
Font Gentium https://software.sil.org/gentium/charset/
Fonts Sanskrit https://www.omniglot.com/bloggle/?p=621
Fonts List http://www.devanaagarii.net/fonts/

Text Shaping Engine Microsoft Uniscribe
https://learn.microsoft.com/en-us/typography/develop/processing-part1
https://learn.microsoft.com/en-us/typography/script-development/devanagari
https://learn.microsoft.com/en-us/typography/tools/volt/
https://www.unicode.org/L2/L2021/21112-deva-cluster-valid.pdf
https://lindenbergsoftware.com/en/notes/issues-in-devanagari-cluster-validation/
https://simoncozens.github.io/fonts-and-layout/features-2.html#mark-positioning
https://learn.microsoft.com/en-us/typography/script-development/devanagari#shaping-engine

https://www.icann.org/sites/default/files/lgr/lgr-4-devanagari-script-05nov20-en.html

Devanagari Scripts (deva) and (dev2) Shaping Engine
https://github.com/n8willis/opentype-shaping-documents/blob/master/opentype-shaping-devanagari.md#distinctions-from-dev2

Text Shaping Engine Microsoft Directwrite
https://learn.microsoft.com/en-us/windows/win32/directwrite/direct-write-portal

Text Shaping Engine Apple Coretext
https://developer.apple.com/documentation/coretext/

Text Shaping Engine Adobe InDesign
https://helpx.adobe.com/in/indesign/kb/shaping-engine-world-ready-composer.html
https://helpx.adobe.com/in/photoshop/using/unified-text-engine.html

Text Shaping Engine Android Chrome Harfbuzz
https://github.com/harfbuzz/harfbuzz

Designing Devanagari Typefaces
https://designwithfontforge.com/en-US/Designing_Devanagari_Typefaces.html

Font Editors
https://fontforge.org/en-US/
https://www.high-logic.com/font-editor/fontcreator
https://glyphsapp.com/
https://www.glyphrstudio.com/
https://www.fontlab.com/

Font Forum
https://typedrawers.com/discussion/3870/attaching-a-devanagari-vedic-extensions-base-glyph-with-a-mark

https://typography.guru/forums/topic/105460-adobe-devanagari-font/
https://typedrawers.com/discussion/4360/indic-shaping-issue-in-devanagari-font

Text Editors
https://www.libreoffice.org/
https://www.microsoft.com/en/microsoft-365/
https://www.latex-project.org/

https://www.lexilogos.com/keyboard/sanskrit_vedic.htm
https://www.w3.org/International/ilreq/devanagari/

Keyboard Editors
https://www.kbdedit.com/
https://www.kbdedit.com/manual/ex23_sanskrit_with_vedic_extensions.html
https://help.keyman.com/
https://help.keyman.com/keyboard/sil_devanagari_phonetic/1.4/sil_devanagari_phonetic
https://ubcsanskrit.ca/keyboards.html
https://kbdlayout.info/KBDINDEV/
https://kevincarmody.com/software/aksharapad.html
https://mywhatever.com/home/sanskrit/vidyut/
https://www.alanwood.net/unicode/vedic-extensions.html

Ashwini Kumar Aggarwal
– Sanskrit Sandhi Handbook – 1st – 2019 –
– The Sanskrit Alphabet with Vedic Extensions – 1st – 2021 –
Devotees of Sri Sri Ravi Shankar Ashram, Punjab.

Epilogue

Sing freely.
Sing from your Soul.
Sing whenever you want.

Offer all to Her and rest deeply.

सर्वे भवन्तु सुखिनः । सर्वे सन्तु निरामयाः ।
सर्वे भद्राणि पश्यन्तु । मा कश्चिद् दुःख भाग् भवेत् ॥
ॐ शान्तिः शान्तिः शान्तिः ॥

When faith has blossomed in life, Every step is led by the Divine.
Sri Sri Ravi Shankar

Om Namah Shivaya

जय गुरुदेव

www.ingramcontent.com/pod-product-compliance
Ingram Content Group UK Ltd.
Pitfield, Milton Keynes, MK11 3LW, UK
UKHW021403190726
13845UKWH00028B/846

9 788195 075485